Blue Mesa Review

Number Seven

The Creative Writing Center
University of New Mexico

BLUE MESA REVIEW　　　　　　　　NUMBER SEVEN

THE MYTHIC SOUTHWEST

EDITOR
David Johnson
EDITORIAL BOARD
Laurie Alberts, Patricia Clark Smith,
Gene Frumkin, Joy Harjo, Sharon Warner
BOOK REVIEW EDITOR
Lee Bartlett
MANAGING EDITOR
Patricia Lynn Sprott
ASSISTANT EDITOR
Steven Pearl
EDITORIAL ASSISTANTS
Rebecca Aronson, Inez Petersen, Gayle Krueger

BLUE MESA REVIEW accepts manuscripts from May through September, and responds by the end of December. Manuscripts received from October through April will be returned unread. Simultaneous submissions or previously published material will not be accepted. The theme for the next issue is *Approaching the Millennium*.

Please send two copies of each manuscript, typed, double-spaced, with your name, address and telephone number (FAX number and electronic-mailing address also appreciated).

BLUE MESA REVIEW
Department of English
University of New Mexico
Albuquerque, NM 87131

phone: 505/277 6347
fax: 505/277 5573
e-mail: psprott@unm.edu

Funding for BLUE MESA REVIEW is provided by the College of Arts and Sciences, University of New Mexico. Please order through the University of New Mexico Press: 1(800)249-7737.

COVER ART　　　　　*River's Edge,* hand-tufted rug by Joan Weissman
COVER DESIGN　　　J.B. Bryan

©1995 The Creative Writing Center / The University of New Mexico
ISBN 1 885290 06

Blue Mesa Review
Number Seven

The Mythic Southwest
  Enrique Lamadrid
  with photos by Miguel Gandert
      La Querencia: Moctezuma
      and the Landscape of Desire   3
  V.B. Price
      Myth and Progress   9
  Luci Tapahanso
      All the Colors of Sunset   17
  Criss Jay
      The Ghost and the Swallows   22
      With a Young Rabbi in Chimayo   24
  Sergio Troncoso
      The Snake   26
  Harvena Richter
      Beginning   37
  Tina Carlson
      Mt. Taylor   39
  Cathryn McCracken
      Midwives   40
  Gabriel Herrera
      No Me Gusta le Chile   48
  Karla Kuyaca
      One For Easy To Talk To   50
      Durango   51
  E.A. Mares
      The Weight of Fallen Angels   52
  Jefferson Adams
      The Rare Capture &
      Transformation of Canyon
      to Body by Fog   66
  Jeanne Shannon
      Three Mornings in the
      Floating World   68
  Sharon Hatfield
      Black Widow   70
  Robert Edwards
      For Joan   73
      Old Oraibi   75

Blue Mesa Review
Number Seven

Mary Helen Fierro Klare
    Doña Fortunata and Andrés
    Cookies, Cuentos
    and Friendship   77

Roberta Swann
    Cochiti Corn Dance   83
    Fire in the Hole   84

Jana Giles
    Lies   85

Trebbe Johnson
    Drought   91

◆◆◆◆◆◆◆

Peter Wild
    Barnyard   102
    Millionaires   103

Albino Carrillo
    Discovering a Christian
    Hymnal: Winter 1980   104

Laurie Kutchins
    The Placenta   106
    Afternoon Along
    the Firehole River   107

José Esquinas
    Cosas, Inc.   109

Jeffrey Lamar Coleman
    Onslaught in the
    Upper Western Hemisphere   118
    Alone in Presence of Air   119

Sören Johnson
    Bus Station, Itea, Greece   121

Erika Lenz
    The Waitress   122

Cody Wasner
    Drawing Blood   124

Amy L. Uyematsu
    In America Yellow
    is Still an Insult   132
    In a Room Named Shimmer   134

John Couturier
    Nervous   135

Blue Mesa Review
Number Seven

C. John Graham
    BEYOND SCIENCE   136

Pauline Mounsey
    COUSINS ONCE REMOVED   137

Mario Materassi
    THE ONE WHO FELL   138

Leilani Wright
    THE DISSOLUTION   142

Craig M. Baehr
    MARKS IN MY SKIN   143

Glenna Luschei
    QUICK   145

Troung Tran
    MY FATHER'S STORY
    MY FATHER'S LEGACY   147

William B. Smith
    AUNT MARGIE IS SUPPOSED
    TO DIE BY CHRISTMAS   148

Henry Rael, Jr.
    WET PAINT   151

Kathleen Spivack
    FROM THE TERRACE   157
    AFTER SUMMER   159

Joanna Brooks
    YOU ASK WHAT I AM
    THINKING ABOUT   161

Lyn Lifshin
    THE DREAM OF THE WHITE BIRD   163

Joe Pitkin
    WATERMELON TREE   164

Thomas Swiss
    MENTAL CHESS   165
    WALKIE TALKIE   166

Robert Masterson
    WORDS IN MY MOUTH,
    DON'T PUT THEM   167
    STEALING CARS FOR
    KELLY ASHNER   169

Carrie Etter
    MCLEAN COUNTY HIGHWAY 39   170

Carl Mayfield
    NOT QUITE AUDEN   171

BLUE MESA REVIEW
NUMBER SEVEN

Bobby Byrd
    THE MEANING OF NORTH DALLAS   173
Enid Osborn
    THE ONE-HANDED MARY   181
Jennifer L. Miller
    THE ALMANAC IS PREDICTING
    A HARSH WINTER   185
Alexis Rotella
    THE CLOCK INSIDE
    MY FATHER BREAKS   186
    RUN FOR ICE   187
Glen Sorestad
    ANOTHER SEPTEMBER SONG   188
Jenny Goldberg
    STREETLIGHTS   189
Iqbal Pittalwala
    RIGHTS   190
Heather O'Shea Gordon
    ABOUT THE AUTHOR   193
Michael Sinclair
    WHEN I DREAM NANCY SPUNGEN   194
Robert Burlingame
    MODERN LOVE I   198
    MODERN LOVE II   199
Jeanne Shannon
    PAVANE   200

BOOK REVIEWS
    Megan Simpson
        HELEN KELLER OR ARAKAWA   204
    Anne Foltz
        DOWNCAST EYES   207
    Jennifer Timoner
        GEORGES BATAILLE   209

CONTRIBUTOR'S NOTES

THE MYTHIC SOUTHWEST

David Johnson

One way to know a place is by its physical data, its statistical tables: geographical location, demographics, mean temperature, median income, average rainfall. This material provides what might be called an *objective* description of a particular region.

Quite a different way of dealing with place is provided by *insiders*, people who have lived and resonated with it, who have touched its spirit and recorded their impressions in journals, poems, letters, stories, art works, and ceremonials.

For hundreds of years, various peoples have traveled to the Southwest, settled here, and responded to its special qualities. One dimension of this mythic landscape is provided by vistas where a vast sweep of space extends outward beyond one's fingertips, mile after mile like an infinite canopy of air, with the light undulating over a forbidding desert floor of sage and mesquite.

Breaking into this horizontal scene are great rock sculptures and buttes, strange fingers of stone and scrub which suddenly erupt out of the plains. Isolated clusters of hills and mountains rise sharply into the sky and then plunge into shadowed canyons and barrancas.

Neither desert nor mountain alone create the unique spiritual quality of the Southwest, but a combination: the parched, often arid land which reaches to the very base of the mountain, joined by rivers, like arteries linking bone to flesh. This confluence of geography dramatizes the mysterious cutting edge between life and death, the great void that is suddenly filled and then emptied again.

Unlike regions of the United States that are neatly plowed in straight lines and domesticated in row houses, the stark and brilliantly illuminated Southwest has traditionally challenged and shaped its inhabitants. Think of those first settlements huddled along the river valleys, tucked away in caves and canyons; those adobe villages that melted into the background, hardly visible to visitors or enemies from a distance. The actual contours of this desert existence suggest the spirit of reconciliation, rather than the more traditional pattern of domination found in other parts of the country.

At the very heart of the religions indigenous to the Southwest are those stories and ceremonials that honor the forces of desert and mountain, that strike bargains with the sources of water and wind, that attend to the voices of the visible and the invisible.

In a special section of this *Blue Mesa Review*, writers explore the spirit of a unique region, what we've called the Mythic Southwest.

LA QUERENCIA: MOCTEZUMA AND THE LANDSCAPE OF DESIRE

Enrique R. Lamadrid
photos by Miguel Gandert

When we are born in *Nuevo México,* our mother literally gives us the light. "*Da luz,*" we say in the language of our Iberian forebears. As soon as our eyes are accustomed to the brilliance, we memorize the features of her face. As we rise to walk upon the earth, we transpose her profile to those first intimate horizons: a house, a road, cottonwoods by a river, a distant line of hills beyond. Because we are human we see faces in the rocks. Clouds are animate visitors to this realm. Trees lift up their arms to greet them as they pass. The river at their feet is a messenger who sings of life and distant oceans. Drink from this stream and you are destined to return to its waters.

Querencia is the place of returning, the center space of desire, the root of belonging and yearning to belong, a destination overflowing with life but suitable to die in, that vicinity where you first beheld the light. *Querencia* is remembrance of harmony, a longing so profound even trees and stones share

MORADA, NEAR PECOS, NM 1989

in its emotion: "*Los palos, las piedras lloran / por verme salir cautiva.*" In the colonial ballads of exile and captivity, a compassionate landscape is moved to tears by human suffering. *Querencia* in collective terms is homeland.

CAMPO SANTO, MARTINEZTOWN, ALBUQUERQUE, NM I 992

In an arid land, home is always by the water. In the most primordial sense, Nuevo México is P'osoge, the Río Bravo, the great river that cuts its verdant course through the desert. Since all human beings need to be by the water, the banks of this river are by definition a contested space. The *Españoles Mexicanos*, as they called themselves, arrived with all the fury and suppressed desire of the Spanish peasant to possess the land. The price of arrogance was paid in blood in 1680 when the Río Grande Pueblos arose and reclaimed their heritage. In the space of a few mestizo generations, the newcomers who sought title to the land were instead possessed by the land. As they became *Nuevomexicanos*, indigenous to this place, the boundaries of the *Campo Santo*, the Sacred Ground, spread past the narrow church yard and the bones of the dead towards valleys, plains, and mountains beyond.

In the center of this sacred landscape are the native and mestizo peoples who have survived the rigors of the northern desert and the cost of each other's desire. They are dancing. From Taos to Sonora, from Chihuahua to Laredo, they step in unison to the insistent but gentle music of drums and rattles, guitars and violins. The fluttering ribbons that hang from their crowns and shoulders are the colors of the rainbow. In proud formation they do battle against chaos, and reenact the terms of their own capitulation. A bull runs wild through their lines. With three-pronged lightning swords they carve the wind in symmetrical arabesques.

Christian souls or Aztec spirits, they dance in graceful reconciliation, now in crosses, now in circles. In their midst a great king receives the counsel of a little girl. She is Malinche. In the south her name is synonymous with betrayal, but she is no traitor here. At the edges of the fray, the grotesque

BAILE DE LOS MATACHINES, SAN ANTONITO, NM 1989

abuelos guard the dancers, make fun of the people, and ridicule the new order. These old men of the mountains taunt and overpower the *toro*. They kill and castrate the *toro*. They cast its seed to the joyful crowd. Have they vanquished evil as the people say or has the savage bull of European empire met its consummation? *Gracias a Dios* it is a mystery, we all agree. Legend says that long ago Moctezuma himself flew north in the form of a bird with bad news and good advice. He warned that bearded foreigners were on their way north, but if the people mastered this dance, the strangers would learn to respect

EL COMANCHE GALENTO, ALCALDE, NM 1993

them, would join the dance and come to be just like them.

In an arid land a tree is precious. Its hospitable shade is also called home. When Colonel Doniphan and the invading American Army sacked Chihuahua in the spring of 1847, they cut down every tree in town. Green firewood is hard to light without kindling. Paper from the State Archives would do. The eerie light of defiant bonfires in the plaza consumed not only shade but history. In the new order, no undocumented claims to the land would be ratified. In the new order, Mexicans without papers would be called illegals, aliens in their own land.

For half of Mexico to become the United States, it had to be naturalized, its history erased. *El Norte* would be transformed into the Great Southwest. In such a huge landscape, this would be relatively easy. Just paint the Mexicans out of the picture. First have them build the railroad. Then give the

EL CERRO, TOME NM I 989

artists free tickets to Alburquerque in exchange for paintings to be printed in the annual Santa Fe Railroad calendar. After the annihilation of the buffalo, after Wounded Knee, Indians were safe. Paint the Indians. Landscapes are safe too, especially if you paint them without people. The quality of the light is magnificent, the vast emptiness that it illuminates. The buildings are incredible too. Paint them. Take a camera. Paint the church at Ranchos de Taos, take a picture of it. In the mysterious light of historical amnesia, it resembles an adobe mushroom miraculously sprung up after a desert cloudburst or the back side of some earth mother nude. Careful not to get any Mexicans in the frame, though.

Some cultural advice to my *compadres americanos*. You also have been born here, by no choice of your own. You also are weary of this emptiness, the obfuscating clarity of this motherless Southwestern light. Come return to *El Norte* and feel the tranquility of the center space. Kindle a new fire, eat some chile and listen to "*Volver, volver*" on the jukebox. Find a Chicano to translate it for you. No regrets. We all speak pretty good English by now. No need to avert your gaze anymore. Take your camera to the *Matachines*. Nobody will mind. Listen to the music. Talk to the people. Contemplate the mystery of cultural survival. Far overhead, Moctezuma still soars, looking for his *Querencia*!

MYTH AND PROGRESS

V.B. Price

Abo, Chaco, Walpi, Old Oraibi, Canyon De Chelly, Keet Seel, Ojo del Padre, and Datil. American nouns like these are as full of depths and possibilities for some of us in the Southwest as Delphi, Lesbos, Arcadia, and Eleusis are to classicists. Keet Seel and Arcadia are shadows of each other, wild places, the haunts of gods, oases in the outback of history that the Myth of Progress would define as futureless, with no progressive potential, archaeological trinkets only slightly more meaningful than Kachinas and Caryatids lathed in Taiwan. And to most people in the commodified cultures of the East and West, the ancient world, and its modern equivalent, the developing world, are in fact museum souvenirs: a plastic scarab; a poured-glass obsidian butterfly; an Anasazi wind chime made of shards. The Myth of Progress, concerned as it is with the material, the technological, and the marketable, doesn't have much room for anomalies like the American Southwest, places it defines as being merely local, of no global significance except perhaps for the various extractive and exploitative industries. Of course, it's different for people who live in such anomalies. For us who see the Southwest as a mythological sanctuary, a place where the past is still alive, ennobling and energizing the present, Keet Seel and Abo and Ojo del Padre are no more mere local color than the Erechtheum or the Omphalos at Delphi. Oraibi, Chaco and Canyon de Chelly embody a tradition whose full meaning has yet to be realized in a possible future in which the planet has been resacralized and the adaptive ingenuity of Southwestern cultures is refigured as a model of ecological sensitivity, humility and common sense.

In the meantime a more brutal view prevails. For corporate America, the Southwest is synonymous with the primitive, the backward, the undeveloped, the unevolved. Lots of potential. Good workers. Cheap labor. Coal, oil, gas, uranium. Lots of scientists. Lots of empty land to be subdivided forever as timber companies clear cut forests. A good place to retire, to build bombs and to bury poison. Lots of potential.

This reductionist, cost/benefit analysis of the Southwest makes clear the difference between two standard views of myth—one as a gross inaccuracy, the other as a psychic reality. The myths of Arcadia or Chaco Canyon, for instance, are living truths of the spirit and facts of the imagination; the Myth of Progress, in this context, is an error in moral accounting, a manipulative falsehood demeaning the Southwest in order to milk it dry.

The ancient Greeks would see a validation of their pessimism in such a progressive view. For them, progress was full of disastrous paradox. What lie ahead was, by definition, debased. Bronze or iron brought disaster and corruption. The golden age was long ago. The Greeks stood with their backs to the future, yearning for a golden age they could no longer see, watching the odious present rush past them, much as a daredevil motorcyclist might ride backward on a long straight stretch of road.

In the Southwest the past exerts a enlivening influence, keeping the devolving present from complete collapse. Here the past is both sublime and subliminal; sensed out of the far corner of our eye, it both transcends the chaotic exploitation of the present, and exists secretly below the historical horizon, below the conscious rim, radiant with the same synaptic light Rodin felt when he described his feelings about the Reims Cathedral, sensed even in the darkness of night: "Its power transcends the senses so that the eye sees what it sees not."

The Pueblo view of history, while not pessimistic, does have harmonies with that of the ancient Greeks. For them, progress is a dubious concept. The desert mind sees cyclical renewal emerging from lower worlds of cyclical corruption. In Chaco Canyon, we know, vividly, this turn-about on the past: the utopian past at once ennobling and wasting away in the terrible ever present. In Chaco, we know the past as an embryo knows its future form. And so it is with the Southwest. It's a place where cycles of decay have not extinguished the presence of the long ago, where the past exists mythologically in the land, in living languages and cultures, in places such as Abo, Chaco, Walpi, Old Oraibi, Canyon de Chelly, Keet Seel, Ojo del Padre, and Datil.

◆

At Abo, in low winter clouds and twilight chill, my hand rubbed and smoothed and traced a mudhead petroglyph on the cold body of the stone. Maybe a thousand years old; that's as long as the Eleusinian mysteries were performed. The mudhead mask was pecked into a huge, smooth slab of black rock above a shallow wash, not 30 feet from the frozen water of the same spring-fed stream that irrigated what is thought to have been the first wheat field planted by Europeans in the New World 400 years ago, the same stream that fed the bean, squash and corn fields of the Anasazi-Tampiro pueblo that had occupied the site since around 900 A.D. The mudhead petroglyph I found was well within mind sight of the soaring cathedral-like ruin of Abo's church, with its dead straight vertical lines of stone rising from the rounded hills as plumb as the right angle lines of lightning petroglyphs just a gaze away from me and the mudhead I'd just found. When I touched the face on the rock, the mudhead mask, I saw not six inches from *my* face the clay-streaked white backs of Hopi mudheads lined up in a kiva in the dead of winter at Walpi in 1969. An instant physical recall of that night when we'd been given refuge in a blizzard during the Bean Dance cycle for uninitiates. A thousand years of life between my fingers on the stone and my eyes in the drumming dark that night when snowflakes fell into the kiva squeezed onto the edge of First Mesa. Life continuous, ever flowing. That Hopi world had lived on from its golden age right though our world with its omnivorous ideas and idiocies, its barbed wire economies and hygienic savageries. I touched the stone in 1995, the past was still alive, sublime, subliminal in me.

◆

I've been chased off the cliffs of Chaco Canyon by lightning at least three times. And almost blown off the edge of Chacra Mesa, near La Fajada Butte, by a swirling April snow storm that appeared as if it had literally crashed through a seam in the sky, smothering the canyon with weather that only gods could like or endure. I never think of Zeus when I'm at Chaco, but I know the lightning is divine, utterly humbling, horrifying, as beautifully clear as the eye of a shark cruising these very cliffs beneath the sea 50 million years ago. Divine lightning will kill you. Yet it is delicate and animal for all its inhuman power when you see it against black clouds before its sound. I'm always transfixed by that sight, suspended for a split second between the present and the future. And then the thunder and the black rain and wind, and the dead fear of more lightning, ancestral memory radiating eons of panic through my skin and brain. Connection with the past is immediate and intimate. Now, or a thousand years ago, or a thousand years from now, the human response to lightning on the way is galloping, roaring terror. If the lightning's close, I head for low ground, which is hard to find on a cliff, running wildly, tossing out coins and keys, tearing off my belt and its metal buckle. Once lightning struck so close to me, the noise and the light were not two seconds apart. I could smell it all around me. I froze. I couldn't move. And then a great gust of damp wind washed over me and sent me hopping and vaulting down the cliff side to an overhang of stone just large enough to protect me from the rain. I brushed some little pebbles aside, hunched down, relieved, and shifted part of my weight to one of my hands which rested on an odd flat surface. I looked down and saw between my fingers the full body of a 14-15 inch fish dead and fossilized before the sharks could get it. It was the best find I'd ever made at

Chaco, and as the sea storm passed by I wedged the fish slab into a higher shelf of stone and hoped it would glide there until the cliff eroded away.

◆

"They never dance at Old Oraibi anymore," the young Hopi woman told me with a sly smile. "But, they do," I protested. "We were there last year." "No you weren't," she said.

Old Oraibi on Third Mesa, some people say, is the oldest continuously inhabited urban setting in North America. Old Oraibi has been closed off and on to white people for some time. And in the early part of this century, a great schism in Hopi resulted in the Oraibian community splitting itself into two "political" parties—those hostile to whites, and those who were friendly. Before we went to the dances at Old Oraibi, a Hopi at the Cultural Center on Second Mesa told us it was permitted, otherwise we wouldn't have known about it at all. We got there around one in the morning. We were the only whites. The Pueblo had looked deserted the day before when we'd explored it, and at night, with no electricity in the city, nor any electric lights on the horizon, we might as well have been in Troy—until the Kachinas sprang out of the darkness loaded with gifts of scallions, apples and candy, frightening us and welcoming us all at once.

That night, we were not allowed to enter the kivas, but we could stand on top of them and look into the light-filled chamber below with its lines of masked Kachina dancers, and the heart beat of the drums echoing underground throughout the mud-walled city. We knew that these very kivas had been used for a millennium, that 50 generations of Hopis had danced and prayed in them. As we felt our way through the adobe canyons and along the sloping, stony avenues of the old city in shadowed moonlight, we knew these streets had been walked by people who had probably made the pilgrimage to Chaco Canyon 800 years before and had returned home enlivened and refortified by the spiritual power of the religious spectacles there at the Great Kiva now called Casa Rinconada.

When the moon departs, the darkness of Old Oraibi is absolute, except for a soft glow coming from the three main kivas. At 3 a.m., frozen, exhausted, exhilarated, and feeling blessed, I thought of the countless others over the centuries who had seen the kivas glowing like rising suns and had been warmed by the knowledge of the dawn to come.

◆

On the steep peninsular outcropping of Walpi, one worries at night of falling off the edge, especially if the cowbell Kachinas are in earshot. The cowbells, held by clan priests accompanying the masked dancers, signify that these Kachinas are represented by holy people who have fasted and are undergoing a special spiritual journey. Even Hopi people are afraid of them. An outsider learns in a hurry that these masked dancers radiate a dangerous power. At the sound of a cowbell nearby, everyone turns his face to the nearest wall until the dancers pass. Once they came so close to us that we had to run behind some buildings in the dead of night and dive under a truck to keep safe. The truck, we found, was parked over a pile of sheep dung and was not three feet from the fenceless edge of the mesa.

An hour and a half drive from Hopi is another edge that beckons fearfully—the intimate, distant, deep edge of Canyon de Chelly, which drops 1000 feet down from the cap of Permian red limestone to the cliff dwellings and pristine meadowed orchards along the banks of Chinle Wash. So seductively deep, so forbidden. And the swallows that roam the canyon updrafts, diving and ascending, urge me to spread my arms and leap effortlessly into the intimate depths. I came close to jumping once when I was in my early twenties. The landscape I saw was mesmerizing, superreal, mythlike, so perfect, so inviolate, so utterly untouchable and safe, I thought the only way I could become a part of it was to join the swallows, to put my whole self into the view before me, to literally give myself over to the canyon. Happily, I'm more afraid of heights than I am lured by inviolable distance. I stepped back from the edge, got down on my belly, and crawled the few feet back to the rim and peered down. I felt secure in the physical truth that snakes can't join the swallows.

◆

There are few places on earth that seem more secure from intrusion than the Anasazi ruin of Keet Seel near Kayenta, Arizona, and the abandoned town of Ojo del Padre on the Rio Puerco west of Albuquerque.

Keet Seel is a cliff dwelling second only in size to the metropolis called Cliff Palace at Mesa Verde. But unlike Cliff Palace, you can't get to Keet Seel in a tour bus. Even as late as the 1960s, adventuring the eight miles on foot or horseback to see Keet Seel was a 19th century experience, and it wasn't hard for me to feel like Schliemann treking off to Troy or Mycenae. Unlike other Anasazi Ruins, Keet Seel was in pristine condition when I saw it. Nothing had been carted away to museums. The Myth of Progress, which commodifies and dioramas the past, had been kept at bay. Navajo guides used by explorers and proto-archaeologists in the late 19th century kept the place a secret for years, saving it from the fate of Betatakin, another huge ruin nearby which was stripped nearly bare for sale to museums. Even today, only the hardy can get to Keet Seel. So walking its streets you can find corn cobs from the 14th century, an occasional pot, and even roof beams intact.

Tsegi Canyon, where Keet Seel is hidden, is an American Arcadia, a wilderness completely free of anything resembling modern life, a lost place where one's imagination can find peace from the suburban cacophony of the machines. In the Mind of the Unknown where all myths merge, Keet Seel and Arcacia *are* shadows of each other, Keet Seel the capital of Aztlán, Arcadia the roaming grounds of Hermes and Pan, the breezy fields of Aphrodite.

◆

In the 1960s, the ghost town of Ojo del Padre was even more isolated than Keet Seel, despite being not 25 miles from Albuquerque on the west bank of the Rio Puerco. In the mid-1990s, the Rio Puerco is on the verge of being colonized by subdivisions and Ojo del Padre is about to be turned under. Perhaps it's poetic justice. Ojo del Padre was an adobe farming town that had been colonized itself. Its ruins have two dominant structures—a jarring two-story, wooden, Queen Anne saloon and gambling hall, and a one-story, one-room adobe morada meeting house and church for the Penitente brotherhood. The two buildings together are evidence of a first prophetic encounter between the Myth of Progress and pristine outback west of Albuquerque. The saloon was as garish as a strip mall. The morada still had profound spiritual integrity. Dark, cool, low to the ground, hidden from the town near the river behind a little hill, the morada radiated humility and devotion even in ruins, a spiritual energy not to be taken lightly by anyone and not to be touched by unbelievers. When I saw it, its only door had been removed, a heavy cross had been dumped in its courtyard, and there was nothing left inside. But I couldn't bring myself to cross the threshold, any more than I could kiss the cheek of a saint I didn't believe in.

◆

A Puebloan myth that tells of the destruction of Chaco Canyon reminds me of the saloon at Ojo del Padre and the gambling mania of modern New Mexico. The myth relates how the great religious complex at Chaco Canyon came to lose its spiritual purity. The devotional culture there had been taken over by greedy overlords and profaned by a lust for gambling. The Kachinas came to warn the people of Chaco that if they didn't stop gaming and revive their religious life, the rain would desert them. Instead of listening to the kachinas, the Chacoans slit their throats and castrated them. The surviving gods left the canyon and never returned, and Chaco dried up and its people were forced into exile. In rarely seen ceremonials today, the War of the Kachinas is re-enacted with masked dancers wearing bladders full of pig blood around their necks and waists. The death of the Kachinas, and the death of Chaco, comes at the climax of the ceremony when the bladders are punctured, and the blood spills out symbolizing the exchange of death for waters wasted on greed.

◆

The Myth of Progress is fickle. It will have nothing to do with Keet Seel, Walpi, or Canyon de Chelly, but it loves the crossroads of Datil just west of the Plains of San Agustin in that rancher's paradise called Catron County. Datil has a history, but its present is where the action is. Datil has one business that I can tell, the Eagle Guest Ranch, which is not a ranch, though it does have rooms for rent. It's mostly a restaurant and a market and gas station, with the best food for miles and among the most interesting conversations anywhere in America. In the Eagle, the unlikely mixing of the myth of the cowboy with the ancient history of stargazing and its practitioners makes eavesdropping an almost cosmically funny experience. At one table, astrophysicists from the Very Large Array radio telescope east on the Plains of San Agustin talk about positioning the VLA's huge cup-shaped antennae, and at another table tired cowboys smoke and complain about the rain and their pickup trucks buried in three feet of mud. The power of technology feels softened at the Eagle Guest Ranch. There's a continuity there of mud and stars. The curiosities of the great Anasazi astronomers, who designed whole urban networks like Chaco Canyon to be vast solar and lunar calendars, merge over smells of wet dirt and steak with the driving inquisitiveness of the modern world's best astronomers. The cowboys too have ancestral roots in the Myth of Progress, roots that follow them to Datil—Plains Indians who hunted and raided into New Mexico and Colorado, Navajo horsemen and shepherds, Apache raiders and stockmen, all as peripheral to the Pueblo core as the cowboys are peripheral to the radio telescopes of the VLA. Datil, for an habitué of cafes like myself, is a sort of mythological relay station in which energy from the past is amplified and pushed on to the future. If there was ever evidence that the field of myth is still perfect with all its potential energy radiating possibility, it's the words I thought I overhead one Christmas season having supper with my family after cutting our trees in the Crosby Mountains. Eating pie and drinking coffee at the Eagle, one fairly scruffy scientist, who looked like a cowboy, said matter-of-factly to another man in a tweed jacket and bolo tie, "there's so little blight in our skies out here." Urban "light blight" I think he was talking about—the same progressive curse that's been missing from the clear night skies of Chaco Canyon and the far back pastures of Catron County since long before the first myth dawned on the questioning human mind.

All the Colors of Sunset

Luci Tapahanso

Even after all this time, when I look back at all that happened, I don't know if I would do anything differently. That summer morning seemed like any other. The sun came up over the mountain around seven or so, and when I went to throw the coffee grounds out, I put the pouch of corn pollen in my apron pocket so that I could pray before I came inside.

During the summers, we sleep most nights in the *cha'aoh*, the shadehouse, unless it rains. I remembered early that morning I had heard loud voices yelling and they seemed to come from the north. Whoever it was quieted quickly, and I fell back asleep. Right outside the *cha'aoh*, I knew the dogs were alert—their ears erect and eyes glistening. Out here near Rockpoint, where we live, it's so quiet and isolated that we can hear things from a far distance. It's mostly desert, and the huge rocks nearby, *tse ahil ah neee*, whale rock and the other rocks seem to bounce noises into the valley. People live far apart and there are no street lights nearby. The nights are quiet, except for animal and bird noises, and the sky is always so black. In the Navajo way, they say the night sky is make of black jet, and that the folding darkness comes from the north. Sometimes in the evenings, I think of this when the sun is setting, and all the bright colors fall somewhere into the west. Then I let the beauty of the sunset go, and my sadness along with it.

That morning I fixed a second pot of coffee, and peeled potatoes to fry. Just as I finished slicing the potatoes, I thought I heard my grandbaby cry. I went out and looked out toward my daughter's home. She lives across the arroyo a little over a mile away. I shaded my eyes and squinted—the sun was already so bright. I didn't see anyone. I stood there awhile listening and looking in her direction. Finally, I went inside and finished fixing breakfast. We were going to go into Chinle that afternoon, so I didn't go over to their house.

Later that morning, I was polishing some pieces of jewelry when I heard my daughter crying outside. My heart quickened. I rushed to the door and she practically fell inside the house. She was carrying the baby in her cradleboard and could hardly talk—she was sobbing and screaming so. I grabbed the baby, knowing she was hurt. When I looked at my graddaughter, I knew the terrible thing that had happened. Her little face was so pale and wet from crying. I could not think or speak—somehow I found my way to the south wall of the hooghan and sat down, still holding my sweet baby. My first and only grandchild was gone.

I held her close and nuzzled her soft neck. I sang over and over the little songs that I always sang to her. I unwrapped her and touched slowly, slowly every part of her little smooth body. I wanted to remember every sweet detail and said aloud each name like I had always done, "*Dii nijaad wolye, shi awee.*" This is called your leg, my baby. I asked her, "*Ni tsiyaa sha?*" and nuzzled the back of her neck like before. "*Jo ka i.*" This time she did not giggle and laugh. I held her and rocked, and sang, and talked to her.

The pollen pouch was still in my pocket, and I put a bit into her mouth as I would have done when her first tooth came in. I put a pinch of pollen on her head as I would have done when she first left for kindergarten. I put a pinch of pollen in her little hands as I would have done when she was given her first lamb, as I would have done when she was given her own colt. This way she would have been gentle and firm with her pets. I brushed her with an eagle feather as I would have done when she graduated from junior high. All this and so much more that could have been swept over me as I sat there leaning over my little grandbaby.

She was almost five months old, and had just started to recognize me. She cried for me to hold her and I tried to keep her with me as much as I could. Sometimes I took her for long walks and showed her everything, and told her little stories about the birds and animals we saw. She would fall asleep on our way home, and still I hummed and sang softly. I couldn't stop singing. For some reason when she was born, I was given so much time for her. I guess that's how it is with grandparents. I wasn't ever too busy to care for her. When my daughter took her home, my house seemed so empty and quiet.

They said that I kept the baby for four hours that morning. My daughter left and then returned with her husband. They were afraid to bother me in my grief. I don't remember much of it. I didn't know how I acted, or maybe that was the least of what I was conscious of. My daughter said later that I didn't say one word to her. I don't remember.

Finally, I got up and gave the baby to them so they could go to the hospital at Chinle. I followed in my own truck, and there the doctor confirmed her death, and we began talking about what we had to do next. Word spread quickly. When I went to buy some food at Basha's, several people comforted me and helped me with the shopping. My sisters and two aunts were at my home when I returned. They had straightened up the house, and were cooking already. Some of my daughters-in-law were cooking and getting things ready in the *cha'aoh* outside. By that evening, the house and the *cha'aoh* were filled with people—our own relatives, clan relatives, friends from school, church, and the baby's father's kin. People came and held me, comforting me and murmuring their sympathies. They cried with me, and brought me plates of food. I felt like I was in a daze—I hardly spoke. I tried to help cook and serve, but was gently guided back to the armchair that had somehow become "my chair" since that morning.

There were meetings each day, and various people stood up to counsel and advise everyone who was there, including my daughter and her husband. When everything was done, and we had washed our faces and started over again, I couldn't seem to focus on things. Before all this had happened, I was very busy each day—cooking, sewing, taking out the horses sometimes, feeding the animals, and often just visiting with people. One of my children or my sisters always came by and we would talk and laugh while I continued my tasks. Last winter was a good year for piñons so I was still cleaning and roasting the many flour sackfuls we had picked. At Many Farms junction, some people from Shiprock had a truckload of the sweetest corn I had ever tasted, so I bought plenty and planned to make *ntsidiigoodii* and other kinds of corn bread. We would have these tasty delicacies to eat in the winter. We liked to remember summer by the food we had stored and preserved.

When we were little, my mother taught all of us girls to weave, but I hadn't touched a loom in years. When I became a grandmother, I began to think of teaching some of the old things to my baby. Maybe it was my age, but I remembered a lot of the things we were told. Maybe it was that I was alone more than I had ever been—my children were grown. my husband passed on five years ago, and since I was by myself and I had enough on which to live, I stopped working at a paying job.

After all this happened, I resumed my usual tasks and tried to stay busy so that my grandbaby's death wouldn't overwhelm me. I didn't cry or grieve out loud because they say that one can call the dead back by doing that. Yet so much had changed, and it was as if I was far away from everything. Some days I fixed a lunch and took the sheep out for the day and returned as the sun was going down. And when I came back inside, I realized that I hadn't spoken to the animals all day. It seemed strange, and yet I just didn't feel like talking. The dogs would follow me around, wanting attention—for me to throw a stick for them, or talk to them—then after awhile they would just lie down and watch me. Once I cleaned and roasted a pan of piñons perfectly without thinking about it. It's a wonder that I didn't burn myself. A few weeks later, we had to brand some colts, and give the horses shots, so everyone got together and we spent the day at the corral in the dust and heat. Usually it was a happy and noisy time, but that day was quieter than usual. At least we had taken care of everything.

Sometimes I dreamt of my grandbaby, and it was as if nothing had happened. In my dreams, I carried her around, singing and talking to her. She smiled and giggled at me. When I awoke, it was as if she had been lying beside me, kicking and reaching around. A small space beside me would be warm, and her scent faint. These dreams seemed so real. I looked forward to sleeping because maybe in sleeping I might see her. On the days following such a dream, I would replay it over and over in my mind, still smiling and humming to her the next morning. By afternoon, the activity and noise had usually worn the dream off.

I heard after the funeral that people were whispering and asking questions about what had happened. It didn't bother me. Nothing anyone said or did would bring my sweet baby back—that was clear. I never asked my daughter how it happened. After the baby's death, she and her husband became very quiet and they were together so much, they seemed like shadows of each other. Her husband worked at different jobs, and she just went with him and waited in the pickup until he was through. He worked with horses, helped build hooghans, corrals, and other construction work. When she came over and spent the afternoon with me, we hardly talked. We both knew we were more comfortable that way. As usual, she hugged me each time before she left. I knew she was in great pain.

Once, when I was at Basha's shopping for groceries, a woman I didn't know said to me, "You have a pretty grandbaby." I smiled and didn't reply. I noticed that she didn't say "*yee*" at the end of "*nisoi*," which would have meant "the grandbaby who is no longer alive." That happened at other places, and I didn't respond, except to smile. I thought it was good that people remembered her.

About four months after her death, we were eating at my house when my sisters gathered around me and told me that they were very worried about me. They thought I was still too grief-stricken over the baby, and that it was not healthy. "You have to go on," they said, "let her go." They said they wanted the "old me" back, so I agreed to go for help.

We went to a medicine woman near Ganado, and she asked me if I could see the baby sometimes. No, I said, except in dreams.

"Has anyone said they've seen her?" she asked. I said that I didn't think so. Then she said, "Right now, I see the baby beside you." I was so startled that I began looking around for her.

"The baby hasn't left," she said, "she wants to stay with you." I couldn't see my grandbaby. Then I realized that other people could see what the medicine woman had just seen. No wonder, I thought, that sometimes when I woke, I could feel her little warm body beside me. She said the baby was wrapped in white.

She couldn't help me herself, but she told me to see another medicine person near Lukaichakai. She said that the ceremony I needed was very old and that she didn't know it herself. The man she recommended was elderly and very knowledgeable and so it was likely that he would know the ceremony, or would at least know of someone who did.

Early in the morning, we went to his house west of Many Farms—word had already been sent that we were coming. The ceremony lasted for four days and three nights, and parts of songs and prayers had such ancient sacred words I wasn't sure if I understood them. When the old man prayed and sang, sometimes tears streamed down my face as I repeated everything after him—word for word, line for line late into the night—and we would begin again at daybreak the next morning. I was exhausted and so relieved. I finally realized what my grief had done. I could finally let my grandbaby go.

We were lucky that we found this old man because the ceremony had not been done in almost eighty years. He had seen it as a little boy and had memorized all the parts of it—the songs, the advice, the prayers, and the literal letting go of the dead spirit. Over time, it had become a rare ceremony, because what I had done in holding and keeping the baby for those hours was not in keeping with the Navajo way. I understood that doing so had upset the balance of life and death. When we left, we were all crying. I thanked the old man for his memory, his life, and his ability to help us when no one else could. I understand now that all of life has ceremonies connected with it, and for us, without our memory, our old people, and our children, we would be like lost people in this world we live in, as well as in the other worlds in which our loved ones are waiting.

The Ghost and the Swallows

Criss Jay

The hill is pregnant with rock
and the calm faces of dead women
buried in final conversation,
men with crooked hands floating under the grass.
The oak and saltbush do what they can
for the scorched bones of a potter
and the horse that could not escape.
Somewhere a spring, and near it the body
of the mission rearing up with its eyes fallen out,
wasps humming in the archway,
the stolen vigas and mud
that had made a temporary heaven of the West.

How alone this empty face in the ruins,
the priest restless with slaughter,
walking the dirt floor,
unable to light the candles
or recall his Latin phrases.
The stars press down on him,
a rain of broken glass,
sharp spear of the moon in his spine.
He hears the dark reminiscing of blood
in the Pecos, still sees the stains of betrayal
washing over the banks at sunrise
and the snakes coiled around
the arms of the crucifix.
He remembers children walking through fire,
and pronghorn that lifted into another sky.

And then the violins,
the strange quartet of Haydn
scratching at his mind
as the last Tewas made their desperate
ending over the mesa.

Every morning he climbs into a window of wind,
every day waiting for the swallows
to swarm over the rusted creek,
syllables darting from the mouths of hollow nests,
wings making their inflections
over pools, in the air writing
downward across the abandoned rocks
as if to let him read whatever
holiness might have been left behind.

With A Young Rabbi in Chimayo

Criss Jay

We left the excruciations of Jesus
hanging on a tree with two squirrels
quarreling over the body,
one trying to steal the crown for a nest.
Blue ribbons twirled off the stations of the cross.
Ants wandered in the wind over the white linen
foraging for crumbs of the Eucharist.

At the river we could smell
the glut of frogs and moist horses in the grass,
the afternoon fires lingering over the orchards.
You wanted to talk about the church,
a perverse sanctuary you called it
of crutches and bloody shoes, the stuffed dolls
with martyred transvestites hung in chiffon and pearls.
You wondered at pilgrims eating dirt
from a hole in the floor,
why soldiers would pin their photographs
to a ghost poured from colored glitter.
You spoke of education, the modern world,
why the children must get out of this valley,
that even the stubbled hills can become anathema.

You seemed to be arguing more with the water
or some absence in the stones
as I turned to walk a little further down the bank.
I wanted only the discourse of trees, to hear
the centuries of supplication still growing in the bark.
I wanted to sit beneath the white doves and the sun
falling over us into the dusk.

I wanted you to look with me
through the sunflowers, past the barbed wire
to an old farmer beside his house,
to imagine why he suddenly let go of his ax
when the bells struck the air,
why he crossed himself
and began to dance like a Matachine,
a scarf of red roses fluttering
from the back of his boot.

THE SNAKE

Sergio Troncoso

The chubby boy slammed the wrought iron screen door and ran behind the trunk of the weeping willow in one corner of the yard. It was very quiet here. Whenever it rained hard, particularly after those thunderstorms which swept up the dust and drenched the desert in El Paso during April and May, Tuyi could find small frogs slithering through the mud and jumping in his mother's flower beds. At night he could hear the groans of the bullfrogs in the canal behind his house. It had not rained for days now. The ground was clumped into thick white patches which crumbled into sand if he dug them out and crushed them. But he was not looking for anything now. He just wanted to be alone. A large German shepherd, with a luminous black coat and a shield of gray fur on its muscular chest, shuffled slowly toward him across the patio pavement and sat down, puffing and apparently smiling at the boy. He grabbed the dog's head and kissed it just above the nose.

"*Ay,* Princey *hermoso.* They hate me. I think I was adopted. I'm not going into that house ever again! I hate being here, I hate it." Tuyi put his face into the dog's thick neck. It smelled stale and dusty. The German shepherd twisted its head and licked the back of the boy's neck. Tuyi was crying. The teardrops that fell to the ground, not on the dog's fur nor on Tuyi's Boston Celtics T-shirt, splashed into the dust and rolled up into little balls as if recoiling from their new and unforgiving environment.

"They give everything to my stupid sister and my stupid brothers and I get nothing. They're so stupid! I always work hard, I'm the one who got straight A's again, and when I want a bicycle for the summer they say I have to work for it, *midiendo.*

I don't want to, I already have twenty-two dollars saved up, Oscar got a bicycle last year, a ten-speed, and he didn't even have anything saved up. He didn't have to go *midiendo.* Diana is going to Canada with the stupid drum corps this summer, they're probably spending hundreds of dollars for that, and they won't give me a bicycle! I don't want to sit there in the car waiting all day while Papa talks to these stupid people who want a new bathroom. I don't want to waste my summer in the hot sun *midiendo,* measuring these stupid empty lots, measuring this and that, climbing over rose bushes to put the tape right against the corner. I hate it. Why don't they make Oscar or Ariel go! Just because Oscar is in high school doesn't mean he can't go *midiendo.* Or Ariel could go too, he's not so small, he's not a baby anymore. And why don't they put Diana to work! Just because she's a girl. I wish I were a girl so I could get everything I wanted to for free. They hate me in this house."

"Tuyi! Tuyi!" his mother yelled from behind the screen door. "*¿En dónde estás, muchacho?* Get over here at once! You're not going outside until you throw out the trash in the kitchen and in every room in this house. Then I want you to wash the trash cans with the hose and sweep around the trash bins outside. I don't want *cucarachas* crawling into this house from the canal. When I was your age, young man," she said as he silently lifted the plastic trash bag out of the tall kitchen can and yanked it tightly closed with the yellow tie, "I was working twelve hours a day on a ranch in Chihuahua. We didn't have any *summer* vacation." As he lugged it to the backyard, to the corner where the rock wall had two chest-high wooden doors leading to the street and a brick enclosure over which he would attempt to dump the trash bag into metal bins, a horrible, putrid smell of fish—he hated fish, they had had fish last night—wafted up to Tuyi's nose and seemed to hover around his head like a cloud.

◆

"*¡Oye, gordito!* Do you want to play? We need a fielder," said a muscular boy, about fifteen years old, holding a bat while six or seven other boys ran around the dead end on San Simon Street, which had just finally been paved by the city. When the Martínez family had moved into one of the corner lots on San Simon and San Lorenzo, Tuyi remembered, there had been nothing but dirt roads and scores of empty lots where they would play baseball after school. His older brother, Oscar, was a very good player. He could smack the softball all the way to Carranza Street and easily jog around the bases before somebody finally found it stuck underneath a parked car and threw it back. When it rained, however, the dirt streets got muddy and filthy. Tuyi's mother hated that, the mud wrecked her floors and carpets. No matter how much she yelled at the boys to leave their sneakers outside they would forget and track it all in. But now there was black pavement, and they could play all the time, especially in the morning during the summer. You couldn't slide home, though, you would tear up your knee.

"*Déjalo*. He's no good, he's too fat," a short boy with unkempt red hair said, Johnny Gutiérrez from across the street.

"Yeah. He's afraid of flies. He drops them all the time in school and *el* coach yells at him in P.E.," Chuy sneered.

"Shut up, *pendejos*. We need a fielder," the older boy interrupted again, looking at Tuyi. "Do you want to play, Tuyi?"

"No, I don't want to. But Oscar will be back from washing the car and I think he wants to play," Tuyi said, pointing to their driveway as he began to walk away, down San Lorenzo Street. He knew Oscar would play if they only asked him.

"*Ándale pues*. Chuy, you and Mundis and Pelon will be on my team, and Maiyello, you have the rest of them. Okay? When Oscar comes we'll make new teams and play over there," he said, pointing to a row of empty lots down the street. "There's more room and we can slide. I'll be the fielder, you pitch, Pelon. And don't throw it so slow!"

Tuyi looked back at them as he walked down the new sidewalk, with its edges still sharp and rough where the 2x4's had kept the cement squared. Here someone had scrawled "J + L 4/ever" and surrounded it with a slightly askew heart when the cement had been wet. Tuyi, no one called him Rodolfo, not even his parents, was happy to have won a reprieve from *midiendo* and from cutting the grass. He was not about to waste it playing baseball with those *cabrones*. He just wanted to be alone. His father had called home and had told his mother to meet him after work today. They were going to Juárez, first to a movie with Cantinflas and then maybe for some *tortas* on 16 de Septiembre Street, near the plaza where they had met some 20 years before. Tuyi had heard this story so many times he knew it by heart.

His father, José Martínez, an agronomy and engineering student at the Hermanos Escobar School, had walked with some of his university buddies to the plaza. There young people in the 1950's, at least those in northern Mexico, would stroll around the center. The boys, in stiff shirts with small collars and baggy, cuffed slacks, looking at the girls. The girls, in dresses tight at the waist and ruffled out in vertical waves toward the hem, glancing at the boys. If a boy stopped to talk to a girl, her friends would keep walking. Or maybe groups would just stop to talk to each other, Tuyi wasn't quite sure. In any case, this is where papa had told him he had first seen his mother, in a white cotton dress and black patent leather shoes. His mother had been a department store model, his father said, and she was the most beautiful woman he had ever seen. It took him, he told Tuyi, five years of going steady just to hold her hand. They were *novios* for a total of eight years before they even got married!

Today they were going to the movies just as they had done so many times before. Papa had told his mother that he and Tuyi would instead go *midiendo* tomorrow, for a project in Eastwood, on the eastside of El Paso, just north of the freeway from where they lived. Mr. Martínez was a construction engineer at Cooper and Blunt in downtown El Paso. On the side he would take up design projects for home additions, bathrooms, porches, new bedrooms, and the like. The elder Martínez had already added a new carport to his house and was planning on adding another bathroom. He would do the construction work himself, on the weekends, and his sons would help. But today he wanted to go to the movies with his wife. They were such a sappy couple.

"*Buenos días*, Rodolfito. Where are you going, my child?" a woman asked, clipping off the heads of dried roses and wearing thick black gloves. The house behind her was freshly painted white, with a burnt orange trim. A large doberman pinscher slept on the threshold of the front door, breathing heavily, its paws stretched out toward nothing in particular.

"*Buenos días*, Señora Jiménez. I'm just going for a walk," Tuyi answered politely, not knowing whether to keep walking or to stop, so he stopped. His mother had told him not to be rude to the neighbors and to say hello whenever he saw them on his walks.

"Is your mother at home? I want to invite her to my niece's *quinceañera* this Saturday at the Blue Goose. There's going to be *mariachis* and lots of food. I think Glenda is going too. You and Glenda will be in 8-1 next year, in Mr. Smith's class, isn't that right?"

"Yes, *señora*, I'll be in 8-1. My mother is at home now, I can tell her about the party."

"You know, you're welcome to come too. It will be lots of fun. Glenda told me how the whole class was so proud of you when you won those medals in math for South Loop School. I'm glad you showed those snotty Eastwood types that a *Mexicano* can beat them with his mind."

"I'll tell my mother about the party. *Hasta luego, señora*," Tuyi muttered as he walked away quickly, embarrassed, his face flushed and nervously smiling. As he rounded the corner onto Southside Street, his stomach churned and gurgled. He thought he was going to throw up, yet he only felt a surge of gases build somewhere inside his body. He farted only when he was sure no one else was nearby. He had never figured out how he had won three first places in the citywide Number Sense competition. He had never even wanted to be in the stupid competition, but Mr. Smith and some other teachers had asked him to join the math club at school, pressured him in fact. Tuyi finally stopped avoiding them with his stoic politeness and relented when he found out Laura Downing was in Number Sense already. He had a crush on her, she was so beautiful, and anyway, they would get to leave school early on Fridays when a meet was in town. Tuyi hated the competition, however. His stomach always got upset. Time would be running out and he hadn't finished every single problem, or he hadn't checked to see if his answers were absolutely right, his bladder would be exploding and he had to tighten his legs together to keep from bursting, or Laura would be there and he would be embarrassed, he couldn't talk to her, he was too fat and ugly, or he wanted to fart again, five minutes to go in the math test.

After he won his first gold medal, all hell broke loose at South Loop. The school had never won before. The principal, Mr. Jacquez, announced it over the intercom after the pledge of allegiance and the club and pep rally announcements. Rodolfo Martínez won? The kids in Tuyi's class, in 7-1, stared at Tuyi, the fat boy everybody ignored, the one who was always last running laps in PE. Then, led by Mrs. Sherman, they began to applaud. He wanted to vomit. After he won the third gold medal on the last competition of the year at Parkland High School, he didn't want to go to school the next day. He begged his parents to let him stay at home. He pleaded with them, but they said no. The day before the principal had called to tell them about what Tuyi had done. He should be proud of himself, his mother and father said, it was good that he had worked so hard and won for Ysleta. The neighborhood was proud of him. His parents didn't tell him this, but Mr. Jacquez had told them that there would be a special presentation for Tuyi at the last pep rally of the year. He *had* to go to school that day. When Mr. Jacquez called him up to the stage in the school's auditorium, in front of the entire school, Tuyi wanted to die. A rush of adrenalin seemed to blind him into a stupor, he didn't want to move, he wasn't going to move, but two boys sitting behind him nearly lifted him up, others yelled at him to go up to the stage. As he walked down the aisle toward the stage, he didn't notice the wild clapping or the cheering by hundreds of kids, he didn't see Laura Downing staring dreamily at him in the third row as she clutched her spiral notebook, everything seemed supernaturally still, he couldn't breathe. Tuyi didn't remember what the principal had said on the stage. Tuyi just stared blankly at the space in front of him and wished and prayed that he could sit down again. He felt a trickle of water down his left leg which he forced to stop as his face exploded with hotness. Thank God he was wearing his new jeans, they were dark blue, nobody could notice anything. Afterward, instead of going back to his seat, he left the stage through the side exit and cleaned himself in the boy's bathroom in front of the counselor's office. The next day, on the last day of school, when the final bell rung at 3:30, as he walked home on San Lorenzo Street with everything from his locker clutched in his arms, he was the happiest person alive in Ysleta. He was free.

◆

Tuyi walked toward the old, twisted tree just before Americas Avenue, where diesel trucks full of propane gas rumbled toward the Zaragoza

International Bridge. He did not notice the Franklin Mountains to the west. The huge and jagged wall of the flat horizon which would explode with brilliant orange streaks at dusk but was now, at mid-morning, just gray rock against the pale blue of the big sky. His shoulders were slumped forward. He stared at the powdery dirt atop the bank of the canal, stopping every once in awhile to pick up a rock and hurl it into the rows of cotton fields around him. He threw a rock against the 30 mph sign on the road. A horribly unpeaceful clang shattered the quiet and startled him. A huge dog, he was terrified of every dog but his own, lunged at him from behind the chain link fence of the last house on the block. The black mutt bared its teeth at him and scratched its paws into the dust like a bull wanting so much to charge and devour its target. At the end of the cotton field and in front of Americas Avenue, Tuyi waited until a red Corvette zoomed by going north and then ran across the black pavement and down the hill onto a perpendicular dirt road which hugged the canal on the other side of Americas. There would be no one here now. But maybe during the early evening some cars would pull up alongside the trees that lined this old road. Trees that grew so huge toward the heavens only because they could suck up the moisture of the irrigation canal. The cars would sit under the giant shade while groups of men, and occasionally a few women, would sit and laugh, drink some beers, throw and smash the bottles onto rocks, just wasting time until dark, when the mosquitoes would swarm and it was just better to be inside. Walking by these trees, Tuyi had often seen used condoms lying flat like flattened centipedes which had dried under the sun. He knew what they were, some stupid kids had brought condoms to school for show and whipped them around their heads at lunchtime or hurled them at each other like giant rubber band bombs. Tuyi had also found a ring once, made of shiny silver and with the initials "SAT" inside. He didn't know anyone with these initials. And even if he had he probably wouldn't have returned the ring anyway: he had found it, it was his. Tuyi imagined names that might fit such initials: Sarah Archuleta Treviño, Sócrates Arturo Téllez, Sigifredo Antonio Torres, Sulema Anita Terrazas, or maybe Sam Alex Thompson, Steve Andrew Tillman, Sue Aretha Troy. After he brought the ring back home and hid it behind the books on the bookshelves his father had built for him, he decided that "SAT" didn't stand for a name at all but for "Such Amazing Toinkers", where toinkers originally referred to Laura Downing's breasts, then later to any amazing breasts, and then finally to anything that was breathtaking and memorable. The sun sinking behind the Franklin Mountains and leaving behind a spray of lights and shadows was a "toinker sun". The cold reddish middle of a watermelon "toinked" in his mouth whenever he first bit into its wonderful juices.

About a half mile up the dirt road, Tuyi stopped, he was at his favorite spot. He shuffled around the trunk of the oak tree and found a broken branch, which he then trimmed by snapping off its smaller branches. In the canal, he pushed his stick into mud, the water was only a couple of inches deep, and flung out globs of mud. He was looking for tadpoles. The last time he had found one, he brought it up to a rock near the tree, its tail was slimy and slick, and found a styrofoam cup which he filled up with water. Under the tree he watched it slither around the cup, with tiny black dots on its tail and a dark army green covering its bulletlike body. After a few minutes, he flicked open his Swiss army knife and slit the tadpole open from head to toe. The creature's body quivered for a second or two and then just lay flat like green jelly smeared on a sandwich. Tuyi noticed a little tube running from the top of the tadpole's head to the bottom and a series of smaller veins branching off into the clear green gelatinous inside. He found what he took to be one of the eyes and sliced it off with the blade. It was just a black mass of more gushy stuff which was easily mashed with the slightest pressure. He cut the entire body of the tadpole in thin slices from head to tail and tried to see what he could see, what might explain how this thing ate, whether it had any recognizable organs, if its color inside was different from the color of its skin. Today he didn't find anything in the mud except an old Pepsi bottlecap and more black mud.

He walked toward the edge of the cotton field abutting the canal. Here he found something fascinating indeed. An army of large black ants scurried in and out of a massive anthole, those going inside carrying something on their back, leaves or twigs or white bits which looked like pieces of bread, and those marching out of the hole following, in the opposite direction, the paths of the incoming. The ants would constantly bump into each other, go around, and then follow the trail back toward whatever it was that kept them busy. How could ants follow such a trail and be so organized? Did they see their way there? But then they wouldn't be bumping into each other all the time. Or did they smell their way up the trail and back home? Maybe they smelled each other to say hello, such as one might whose world was the nothing of darkness. Tuyi wondered if these black ants were somehow communicating to each other as they scurried up and down blades of grass and sand and rocks, never wavering very far from their trails. Was this talking audible to them? Was there an ant language? There had to be some sort of communicating going on among these ants. They were too organized in their little marching rows for this to be random. Maybe they recognized each other by smell. He thought this might be the answer because he remembered what a stink a small red ant had left on his finger after he crushed it between his finger tips. This might be its way of saying, "Don't crush any more red ants or you'll be smeared with this sickly sweet smell," although this admonition could be of no help to one already pulverized. It was for the red ants of the future. Maybe, ultimately, red ants didn't care if any one of them died as long as red ants in general survived and thrived without being crushed by giant fingers. Anyway, this would make red ants quite different from humans, who were individualistic and often didn't really care about anyone else except themselves. For the most part, humans were a stupid, egotistical mob. Tuyi decided to find out if black ants could somehow talk to each other.

Finding one ant astray from the rest, Tuyi pinned it down with his stick. This ant, wriggling underneath the wooden tip, was a good two feet from one of the trails near the anthole. Its legs flailed wildly against the stick, tried to grab on to it and push it off while its head bobbed up and down against the ground. After a few seconds of this maniacal desperation—maybe this ant was screaming for help, Tuyi thought—six or seven black ants broke off from a nearby trail and rushed around the pinned ant, coming right to its head and body and onto the stick. They climbed up the stick, and just before they reached Tuyi's fingers he let it drop to the ground. It worked. They had freed their friend from the giant stick. Tuyi looked up, satisfied that he had an answer to whether ants communicated with each other. Just about halfway up from his crouch he froze: a rattlesnake slithered over the caked desert floor next to the earth churned up by the rows of cotton, about three feet away. He still couldn't hear the rattle, although the snake's tail shook violently a few inches from the ground. Tuyi was a little hard of hearing, probably just too much wax in his head. The snake stopped, it had been crawling toward him, and now it just stopped. Its long, thick body twisted tightly behind it while its raised tail still shook against the hot air. He didn't move, he was terrified, should he run or would it spring toward him and bite him? He stared at its head, which swayed slowly left to right. It was going to bite him, he had to get out of there, but if he moved it would certainly bite him, and he couldn't move fast enough to get out of its way when it lunged. He was about to jump back and run when he heard a loud crack to his right. The snake's head had been torn off, orange fluid was splattered over the ground. The headless body wiggled in convulsions over the sand.

"God-damn! Git outta' there boy! Whatcha doin' playin' w'th a rattler? Ain't ye got no *sense*? Git over here!" yelled a burly, red-headed Anglo man with a pistol in his hand. There was a great, dissipating cloud of dust behind him, his truck's door was flung open. It was an INS truck, pale green with a red siren and searchlights on top of the cabin.

"Is that damn thing dead? It coulda' killed you, son. *¿Hablas español?* Damn it," he muttered as he looked at his gun and pushed it back into the holster strapped to his waist, "I'm gonna haf 'ta make a report on firin' this weapon."

"I wasn't playing with it. I was looking at ants. I didn't see the snake."

"Well, whatcha doin' lookin' at ants? Seems you should be playin' somewhere else anyways. Do you live 'round here, boy? What's yer name?"

"Rodolfo Martínez. I live over there," Tuyi said, pointing at the cluster of houses beyond the cotton fields. "You work for the Immigration, right? Can you shoot *mojados* with your gun or do you just hit them with something? How do you stop them if they're running away?"

"I don't. I corner the bastards and they usually giv' up pretty easy. I'm takin' you home, boy. Git in the truck."

"Mister, can I take the snake with me? I've never seen a snake up close before and I'd like to look at it."

"Whatha hell you want w'th a dead snake? It's gonna stink up your momma's house and I know she won't be happy 'bout that. Shit, if you wanna take it, take it. But don't git the thang all over my truck. Are you some kinda' scientist, or what?"

"I just want to see what's inside. Maybe I could take the skin off and save it. Don't they make boots out of snake skin?"

"They sure as hell do! Nice ones too. They also make 'em outta elephant and shark, but ye don't see *me* cutting up those an'mals in my backyard. Here, put the damn thang in here." The border patrolman handed him a plastic Safeway bag. Tuyi shoved the headless carcass of the snake into the bag with his stick. The snake was much heavier than he thought, and stiff like a thick tube of solid rubber. He looked around for the head and finally found it, what was left of it, underneath the first row of cotton in the vast cottonfield behind him. As the INS truck stopped in front of the Martínez home on San Lorenzo Street and Tuyi and the border patrolman walked up the driveway, the baseball game on San Simon stopped. A couple of kids ran up to look inside the truck and see what they could see.

"They finally got him. I told ya' he was weird! He's probably a mojado, from Canada. They arrested him, *el pinchi gordito.*"

"Shut up, you idiot. Let's finish the game. We're leading 12 to 8. Maybe *la migra* just gave him a ride. Why the hell would they bring 'em back home if he was arrested?"

"Maybe they don't arrest kids. He's in trouble, wait til his father gets home. He's gonna be pissed off. They're gonna smack him up, I know it."

"Come on! Let's finish the game or I'm going home. Look it, there's blood on the seat, or something."

"I told ya, he's in trouble. Maybe he threw a rock at the guy and he came to tell his parents. Maybe he hit 'em on the head with a rock. I tell ya, that Tuyi is always doin' something weird by himself. I saw him in the canal last week, digging up dirt and throwing rocks. He's *loco*."

"Let's go, I'm going back. Who cares about the stupid *migra* anyway."

◆

"*Ay, este niño*, I can't believe what he does sometimes. And what did the *migra* guy tell you, was he friendly?" asked Mr. Martínez, glancing back at the metal clanging in the back of the pickup as he and his wife pulled up into the driveway. The moon was bright tonight. Stars twinkled in the clear desert sky like millions of jewels in a giant cavern of space.

"Oh, Mr. Jenkins was *muy gente*. I wish I could've given him lunch or something, but he said he had to go. He told me Tuyi wanted to keep the snake. Can you believe that! I can't even stand the thought of those things. I told Tuyi to keep it in the backyard, in the shed. The bag was dripping all over the kitchen and it smelled horrible. I hope the dog doesn't get it and eat it."

"It looks like everyone's asleep. All the lights are out. Let me get this thing out of the truck while you open the door. Do you have your keys? Here, take mine.

"I'm gonna put it in the living room, *está bien*? That way we can surprise him tomorrow. *Pobrecito*. He must've been scared. Can you imagine being attacked by a snake? This was a good idea. I know he'll be happy. He did so well in school too."

"Well, if it keeps him out of trouble, I'll be happy. I hope he doesn't get run over by a car, though," said Mrs. Martínez while pouring milk into a pan on the stove. Only the small light over the stove was on, and that was nearly covered up as she stood waiting for the milk to bubble. "*¿Quieres leche?* I'm going to drink a cup and watch the news. I'm tired but I'm not really sleepy yet."

The house was quiet except for the German shepherd in the backyard who scratched at the shed door, smelling something powerful and new just beyond it. Princey looked around, sniffed the floor around the door, licked it, and after trotting over to the metal gate to the backyard lay down with a thump against the gate, panting quietly into the dry night air. Inside the house, every room was dark except for the one in the back corner from which glimmered the bluish light of a television set, splashing against the white walls in sharp, spasmodic bursts. In the living room, a new ten-speed bicycle, blue with white stripes and black tape over the handlebars, reclined against its metal stop.

Some tags were still dangling from its gears. The tires needed to be pressurized correctly because it had just been the demonstration model at the Wal-Mart on McCrae Boulevard. It was the last ten-speed they had.

BEGINNING

Harvena Richter

Eden a myth? But feel that leaping
of mind and memory when we find
the path by fruiting trees,
the well of knowledge,
and wearied, seek a shady spot
to eat an apple.

That perfect sphere,
    spilling a sweet tartness,
is no sin signal. Eden knows
no crime nor punishment,
is lush orchard and river land,
sustaining angels.
They wave to us like old-time
    family members
when we slide down the ridge
dividing bone from marrow.
And there, as we remembered,
are the four rivers rising,
the cloud-hung mountain,
    and in the garden
the unrepeated rose.

Why make an ending
when beginnings are much better?
There is no Hell nor Heaven—
we return to our source,
small rivulets
running uphill in sunlight to the spring.
We sense which way to go—
    any mongrel cell
maps out the journey without our asking.
The geography of Eden
lies contoured in each gene.

For we are all unfallen,
undescended daughters,
unsired sons,
begotten on the nether side
    of the sword,
behind us on the hill
the four rivers rising,
and on the unthorned vine
    the unrepeated rose.

Mt. Taylor

Tina Carlson

What we hope for
is a mountain,
frozen across a chilled desert.
The sign says 'Gooseberry Trail'
and we follow through aspen
bare and thin as fine hair.
It is on grasses,
frayed and blown
that we slow and sleep
for the first time in days.
My body is windy,
knotted with confusion.
Above, the spruces huddle
blue as a bruise,
thick and silent.

We climb across the black slag of basalt,
snow clutched in its blisters.
Ravens laugh in huge flocks.
On the top, we pry the metal box
its thin messages wait like babies
to be held. They tell us:
'God lives' and 'I am dying
but I haven't told Eddie yet'.
We scribble our prayers on blue paper
and start down in the frayed, grey hours.
What we hope for remains hidden,
but so close, like winter,
we can smell it.

Midwives

Cathryn McCracken

I had no intention of staying that day. Her mother was in there with her, and the hospital had arranged for extra chairs for all the visitors. The curtains were open and it was about four o'clock, the sun starting to slant, the windows on the west side of the room with their cheap yellow curtains waving a little.

Springtime, and everything was covered in the usual mud. Carol's mother was from California and wore enviably clean shoes. I noticed that, coming as I did from Hondo in my filthy pickup. Sometimes in April we can't get out at all, have to get Al's tractor just to make it past the driveway. Taos is really a mess in April.

Carol was lying on her bed, circled up halfway and talking to someone else, but when I came in she stopped and looked at me. Her thin face was thinner, and she couldn't move very much any more except one arm and her mouth. A talker, and somehow she had managed to keep that till the last.

So I sat and felt stupid, the usual waste of time hospital visit. I really loved her, we were pregnant together, we hauled water and lived in mud houses and chewed philosophies at countless potlucks. Not so recently she had confided she thought she was pregnant again, by the new guy, and that she was having morning sickness. Kept throwing up. And that he had introduced her to anal sex and should she marry him and move to Oregon or what?

"Sing to me." The words were as emphatic as ever, her mouth almost a slash in yellowing skin and her eyes held mine in clean triumph above the bedsheets. Ignore this ugly, unfortunate mistake, they told me, and help me get through all this weirdness. Ok, I whispered back, telepathically.

"Swing low, sweet chariot, coming for to carry me home.

Swing low, sweet chariot, coming for to carry me home."

I watched her eyes close at the second verse, her breathing coming shallow and quiet, and into the homestretch of the song, I figured it wouldn't hurt to repeat it. I thought she must be asleep, so quiet and small in the blinding white of the hospital bed.

"Sing me a different song." Just a touch of asperity, and her mother whispered that it had been almost four hours since the last morphine.

"She gets real bad the last half hour."

Now I knew why people went to church. It was to learn the hymns. But I had been Unitarian and the only stuff I knew was in four-part harmony or based on the Dorian mode. Fun stuff, but I couldn't pull it off alone.

"Two roads diverged in a yellow wood . . . " Yes, this has a melody, but she reached up a weak, impatient hand, and ordered me.

"Sing Rock of Ages. Like when I was little."

I did it, with her mother whispering the words to me at the end of each verse and we got through that well enough and long enough for the next shot to come.

"Don't go." They gave her the shot in her hip, had to turn her over to do it. The bones were stuck way out, like a relief map of a woman's skeleton. I stayed.

"Go have a break," I told her mother. "I'll watch in here."

Something was happening and I didn't want any company while I tried to figure it out. I remembered the baby she lost, two months before I had mine. Hers was a girl, too, who swam around so much she tied the cord in a knot. Strangled inside her mother's womb, and then Carol had to carry her around for a month, knowing she was dead, everyone patting her belly and smiling and doing all that cheery mother stuff to her. And the dead baby inside rotting, and then that sad labor, which finally was done. And her divorce, and her new job at the plant nursery.

This hospital, I thought, what can it possibly provide for her? There are no goats, no dances, no potlucks, no plants, no children here. Nothing for us to do while we wait. For melanoma, the fastest of cancers, the thing which had been causing her morning sickness instead of a new baby.

To pass the time I started singing again. After about half an hour of "wearing your long wingfeathers as you fly," I heard a sharp noise of annoyance.

"Stop it, can't you?" Carol was still hunched like a question mark, but she was facing toward me instead of away. In her eyes was a big question. I knew better than to try to answer it for her, though. Carol had no hope at all. Some people thought that was strange. Later, there was a big funeral and people mourned her in the usual unhappy ways, but I don't think very many understood why she wouldn't fight it. She could have stayed in Albuquerque and done the chemo thing. It might have worked, at least the doctors thought so.

"You have to help me, Marie." She smiled, the smile of a healthy thirty-four year old woman with vitality and guts.

"And those old peyote songs are just not that great the thirty-third time around." I laughed because we had been in the tipi the first time together, trying to hold on to our stomachs through the endless rounds of repetitive singing. I went over to the bed, reached out to hold her hand.

In two months she had gone from a normal, healthy person to a piece of frozen meat in a hospital, only the brain and the mouth and one arm still alive. And I don't think a freight train could have stopped it. So the only thing Carol cared about was getting it over.

"I've got to go home." I told her. "Anyway, I don't think I know any more hymns. I'll practice again for tomorrow." It was hot in there, and something smelled.

"Please." It was not a request.

Her mother came in again, with a big bunch of lilacs, the sweet Persian kind that grow practically wild all over Taos and bloom in huge heaps of lavender profusion in the middle of April. She had yellow roses, too, and these I recognized from the bush at the edge of Carol's yard in Hondo, small tea roses with a slight, windy fragrance.

She reached over me to kiss her daughter and to set the bunches of flowers on the bedstand, where they rocked precariously. She was very California in her neat cotton pants and matching top. Carol's face was bunched up and unhappy in the streaming light from the window. I knew that I had to get out of there soon. But I hugged her first, and that's when I noticed it. Almost then I just blurted everything out. You know, what the hell is rotten in here? But I knew, very surely, exactly what was underpinning the sweet reek of lilacs, the delicate tenderness of yellow roses, even Carol's mother's used-to-be-a-teacher perfume.

I said good-bye, practically ran out the door. Up until then it had been ceremonial, friendly. But my nose told the rest of me what was really going on, and even more exactly, it told me when. So I got my muddy feet under my old jeans and I hugged her Mom and told her good-bye. Carol was looking meaner and yellower as the light slid down the wall opposite the window, and I knew that she was going to need another shot pretty soon. So I had some time.

I drove too fast on the way home. My legs were shaky on the pedals and my stomach was unhappy. It was fear, but it was anticipation, too. I took the ten highway miles to Hondo fast, savoring the clean beauty of Indian land without buildings or trash. I had seen Pueblo men out in their pickups just the other day, removing junk from the side of the road, shaking their heads like ravens at a funeral, patiently removing the ugliness of modern civilization, with its lack of attention to the details of beauty.

The sun was still yellow when I got home. I took a bath in the huge clawfoot tub I had scrounged from another adobe down the road, looking out the window at the western sky. Streaky clouds, high, white, patiently thin, were holding in patterns over the Tres Piedras mountains. My visiting mother-in-law was asleep, after patiently killing two jars full of flies in an effort to participate in our alternative lifestyle. I didn't have the heart to tell her how many more were waiting in the walls to hatch.

I washed, rinsed, dried, dressed, each action careful, movements rather more deliberate than usual, almost prayerful. I held my mind blank, no questions, humming the same hymns over and over that I had sung earlier. Curled the hair around my fingers, put on a little perfume, a quiet peaceful one, wore my good denim skirt and cowboy boots and a white blouse. Dressing up for an event.

The road back into town was full of graceful curves, lit as if from within by moonlight. Not a full moon, nothing as obvious or symbolic as that, but a quarter waning moon, its little sliver nevertheless enough light to drive by. My headlights were on the fritz, of course. I was lucky the weather was warm; the heater was completely broken.

On the way I sang some more: Sufi songs learned up at Lama mountain, full of odd syllables and tonal shifts, bits of melody repeated at odd intervals. At the Lama Foundation on Sundays I went up to dance with all the religious nuts who were living off the land (with the help of healthy pocketbooks and Ram Dass' permanent allocation from the sales of *Be Here Now*). I made fun of it, but the singing and dancing were the best praying I have ever had.

In the hospital parking lot I noticed the fancy, clean motorhome was dark. It was about eight o'clock and Carol's parents were probably still in the room. Her father had the ability to disappear, you forgot to notice him, as he melted into the stillness of walls and sheets, his thin lined face a gift from generations of rural Okies, one of whom had migrated to California during the Dust Bowl days. I tried to remember how he looked but couldn't, even though he had been in the room earlier.

It wasn't cold yet, but the wind was moving towards it. Day temperatures held over for an hour or two. The Sangre De Christos looked sharper-toothed than usual behind the Dairy Queen. A quiet Tuesday night, all of the local maniacs still home at supper.

I left the pickup in the west lot, farthest away from Carol's parents' trailer. Instinct. It must have been instinct that kept trying to flood my system with memories, with expectations. I kept thinking about John, Carol's husband, with his rock and roll good looks and his stingy personality and all those goats. Only in Taos would you find someone trying, seriously, to earn a living with forty goats and a house without electricity or water. John was famous for throwing away milk rather than reducing the price or making a trade.

But he was a beautiful man, tall, with the long clean muscles of a surfer, a head of silky dark hair and a face like Jesus only sexier. A soulful guy if you counted his troubles as worthy. For a long time Carol had.

The people at the front desk let me in easy, no stuff about visiting hours. I guess they knew it wouldn't be a problem for much longer. And this was Taos; even in the hospital there was a consideration for process, for the human side.

When I got in there, Laura was already sitting in the corner. Of course we knew each other. Another midwife. And Carol's Mom was standing next to the bed, adjusting the corners of the blanket. Carol was wide awake, plumped up again in the middle of the morphine cycle, so we could expect to hang out for at least a couple of hours.

"You don't really need to be here you know." Carol's mother had given up trying to learn the names of everyone who came in. I could tell she didn't want us there, didn't really want to share. It was like she was making the corners so tight on the sheets that the bad couldn't get in. I could see her doing it, understood it even, but I hoped that we could talk her into going to bed. It is hard to die with your mother holding on to your nightgown.

Her Dad looked over at Carol, lying curled up like a little seahorse in the big white sheets, her face long and horsey in what was now artificial light. She looked yellow and sort of crinkly, like those sheets of fancy dough you use to make baklava.

I remembered how greedy she always was for sweets. A pleasure-lover, she always went for the goodies. Men and potluck dinners. And desserts.

I grabbed her mother's hand.

"Look, I can see you have plenty of help. I'll just wait out here in the hall."

Maybe she noticed my feet, in their clean cowboy boots, or the white shirt or my hair. Hell, maybe she could smell the difference. Though I doubt that, because she had been in there with Carol and the lilacs most of the day.

"I could really use a break." She said it graciously, dissipating my dislike instantly, arousing an overwhelming urge to cry and pat her on the back like a hurt kid. But this was a hurt which wouldn't rub away with a little ice or even a long, soulful hug. And she was getting in the way.

"We'll call you if anything happens."

Carol had her eyes open, intelligence still riding the pale blue irises. So patient. And Laura just sat in the corner, looking at her large white hands, which I had seen pull the top of a baby's head out, stretching the muscles around the perineum a little bit at a time, like pulling pizza dough when you don't want to break any connections. I guess she had learned how to wait. Carol's mother stood looking back and forth between the three of us. Out of control, a little bewildered. Wanting to trust, though, or for a miracle to rise up out of the floor and rescue her baby.

"It's O.K. Really."

I patted her shoulder just a little, real quick, California-style and stood back, making myself quiet, holding in the little flutter in my stomach that told me big business was going on here, even if there was nothing much to see on the surface.

With a glance at her husband that told me just how out of her depth she really was, she went through the open door, turning back to look over her shoulder at the masses of lilac, at the crippled shape of her daughter in the bright bed. Then she sighed, the quietest little outbreath, and left quickly.

"I expect she'll see to supper now."

That was the only thing Carol's dad had to say that night.

We closed the windows about nine. The mesa wind had caught up with sundown and started making its rounds by then, and the thin edge of its blowing held the scents of sage and dirt. Carol and I had a long conversation about quilts, the advantages of basting the seams, how to hold the corners in so that everything comes out in the corners; we even talked about chintzes and calico. She gave me a recipe for orange chicken that I make to this day, a Chinese thing that uses the chopped up peel and little red chilis. Everything felt slow and immense and at the same time irrelevant.

At ten Deena showed up, a newer midwife, looking young and fancy in a long, tiered and embroidered skirt. Real hippy duds. And as soon as she entered the room, I could feel the energy, like a big twister, start to wind around and gather, pulling away, running back and forth, and the quiet imminent patience of the evening was lost. Gathered up into it, we looked at each other's faces, Deena and Laura and I, novices, wondering what we were supposed to do.

Carol was sleeping by then, about two-thirds of the way between shots. Her breathing changed about ten thirty, all of a sudden, into something that sounded almost like a car engine before it throws a rod. A hard, pumping, want-to-break sound. You could practically see this giant piston shoving up from her stomach to her chest like a huge arm. Her whole body went hard with each stroke and then melted in between them. Just like contractions.

It happened for a while, as the three of us sat there watching, and then it stopped. I looked over at her father, who sat on the hard wooden chair as if he had been born there. The man was an expert at waiting. No expression passed between us, but I could tell he had been listening. He seemed to know what was coming, better than any of us did. But we went with our instincts, anyway. There was a familiarity about this.

Laura went up to feel for a pulse, and when her fingers touched Carol's wrist, a little shock seemed to run through her and the piston breathing started up again, even louder, hoarser, but more shallow this time. Just like a machine trying its damnedest to break down. And she had cold fine sweat on her forehead. Laura just stooped over to look at her face, brushing strands of honey-blonde hair over her nose, before returning to her seat. She didn't shrug, but I felt it happen just the same.

I put my hand on Carol's forehead, like you do when a baby is restless in its sleep.

Deena reached into her bag, the inevitable dyed Mexican, ecologically sound string bag, and took out a big bunch of cedar branches. She was into the Native American thing. Went to lots of peyote meetings, rites, had even been invited to Blue Lake one time for something secret and prayerful.

The cedar is really juniper, but everyone calls it cedar anyway. People use it in their cookstoves, a fine-grained, hard-burning, easy to split wood that comes apart in long, red pieces like a painting by Georgia O'Keefe or a perfect sunset. It's aromatic, deep and quiet to the nose, and I hear they make some sort of tea with it to cure colds.

Right now Deena was lighting the branches, one at a time, pausing at each little juncture of needles to murmur syllables, chanting open-voweled sorts of things, like I'd heard at the peyote meeting. The smoke came up in a kind of flourish over her head and she fanned it in big slow sweeps over Carol, singing "*Ah...eee...sana....ma...eee...oooh...na.*" Her voice had a little wiggle in it, like she couldn't quite decide which was the right note. It wasn't melodic at all, and she sang so quietly you wouldn't have thought it was very important, except that the room caught the sounds somehow and sent them back again, in a little visual shimmer like the one that makes mirages happen on dusty roads in a hot summer, or that changes the air over a stove when you're cooking food.

My hand felt light on Carol's forehead like a leaf when all the green has dissolved. Just a small, veined reminder of springtime. The sweat was gone, she felt hot, smoky, separate. I started to talk to her, making it up out of cedar and my own mind, because the room had a wind in it that didn't come from the outside. Blowing the smoke up and out.

"It's all right. Let go. Float it up . . . see? There . . . follow that wind . . . they'll catch you at the other end. " A sensation of falling. Endless.

"Don't be afraid." Shaking in the middle of my stomach like a small earthquake was happening there, but my hand was light, leaflike and the room as quiet as a desert night.

"*Taa....sa....ooooo....ta....sa....oooooo....*" Deena's voice ended in a low quaver, trailing off between two notes and drifted immediately into the smoke. I saw that Deena and Laura were holding hands, and felt Deena's hand take mine.

Water has a feeling like that. And sand. Large amounts of substance without mind, but full of emotion. The room was like a vast container, emptied even of the possibility of sound. Tidal drifts passed silently, dunes rested in indefinite heat, the tiniest breeze fluttered between breaths.

We sat. I could feel a sucking, like a whirlpool, but shaped more like round darkness, the hole at the top of the tipi. You couldn't see it, but it surrounded. It had wet walls and some sort of destination. My hand on Carol's forehead had disappeared. The room held at pause.

Lights and a choking. Hard. Bright. White and loud and voices.

"She's not breathing!" The slamhammer arm up through her chest just twice again and the nurse's face above her grim as she fitted on the face mask and set the oxygen going. Such a hard thing to do and so silly! Carol's last breath choked out and then she held a limpness so implicit that it was obvious. Even to the nurse.

"I'm sorry." Nodding to us. The machine to the side again, gone to get the doctor. Making sure.

I quieted the lights, turned to look at her father, at his patient Okie's mouth and the lines around it, accepting, almost glad. The three of us sat holding hands again. No more smoke, no rivers, no ancient dunes, just a room in white and the small curl of her gone out of it, finally, in as much comfort as we could provide.

I've seen the tunnel in dreams. Wet, black, muscled something. Can feel it waiting there, for me.

We spent the night washing her; that was allowed. By morning she was cold, waxy, and I had to go off somewhere to help pour a foundation. They buried her up on the mesa in an Indian blanket. Hundreds of people, a lot of fear about why and because. Laura had to go to a birth; I heard it was a good one, later.

Deena moved to Seattle the next year, got married to a lumberjack. Laura still makes her living delivering babies.

The yellow roses bloom every year at Carol's old house. Sometimes I make the long climb up to Michael Duncan's land to find her grave, out among drifts of sage and clover, but not often, anymore. Her kid moved in with her father, who is a jeweler, and I hear she's a wild one.

Just once, I dreamed about her, in my house, gone to a room I had never seen before. She was sleeping there, on a fancy quilt, sleeping so peacefully that I hadn't the heart to wake her. I tiptoed quietly out and closed the door.

No Me Gusta el Chile

Gabriel Herrera

zoot-suiters, lowriders, *pandillas*
mi cultura pero trucha ese
you ain't my brother
you are not of my brown race, *mi raza*
Tonatiuh is my god not a mercedes and gold jewlery
"*Corrale la migra*" though i'm not a foreigner and those words don't apply
but I don't feel american I feel mexican-american on a standardized test

mariachis, chile, frijoles, chile, tostadas, chile, can you make tortillas, chile,
are your parents from mexico, chile, do they deal drugs, chile,
why don't you have an accent, chile, are you in a gang, chile,
you're that smart, chile, can you sit on the other side of the restaurant, chile,
look at those dirty Mexicans, chile,
why don't you go back to mexico, chile,
you don't eat chile, chile

no llores mamá yo se que tu trabajo es duro
y el güero no se precupe con tus problemas
pero dios te bendiga y la virgen de guadalupe te protega

those men in the green trucks
go back, go back
i am back
take the indian out take us out
and put us back
we'll steal your land
it was once ours when the nation came to rise
and can i pick your oranges can i pick your grapes on a hot summer day
from 5:30 in the morning till the sun goes down
don't cry or give me any *limosna*
i am of proud people and i accept nothing
merely your ear to hear what truths i speak

in a pot my *abuelita* used before granpa died she put the chile
verde rojo lo que sea
but i don't like that chile not at all
but can i change the recipe can i take the chile out
but what is to be left nothing.

One For Easy To Talk To

Karla Kuyaca

My heart is up
    at the Mountain Dance
My soul rides
    in a wagon,
        I'm wandering
this river, getting old
    and getting fat.
No I don't want to marry
    you old man and
I don't want to marry you
    neither. Maybe
I'll marry that old black
    bear that scared
my mother-in-law and me.
    He'll eat me up
and won't shit me out
    until he gets up
to the Mountain Dance camp
    in some old wagon rut.
He'll be a medicine bear
    so I'll be healed
then I'll come back and
    marry all you guys.

DURANGO

Karla Kuyaca

The visor says the driver is blind
but the road is in braile.
I trusted him but he dropped me off
at the KOA with nothing to get a grip on.
Tourists all around me won't look, but
that kid is staring. "Someone fell from the
Indian caves today." He says quietly. "Were
you there?"
I can't tell him. I can't say. I can't see
but I'm looking
for the opening to the other world.
If I can't find it soon...
can't find it soon...
I will put on Burmuda shorts, and sun glasses.
Sit by the pool.

The Weight Of Fallen Angels

E. A. Mares

for Harold Cupp

I

Forehead slammed his head one more time into Panzón right between and slightly above his eyes. Everyone called him "Forehead" even though his real name was Gabe because he was the champion head-butter of Saint Anthony's Elementary School. He was probably even the champion head-butter of Valle Vista, maybe even of Texas. You couldn't stand up to Forehead's brutal butts. No fifth grader could. Nobody could. Certainly not Panzón.

Augustín watched the fight in silence. He was too small for this sort of contest and he was glad for that. But he felt sorry for Panzón and thought the head-butting might be dangerous for both of his friends. Although it was hard to imagine anything hurting Forehead. Augustín, thinking, thinking all the time, watched every move that his two friends made. He was ready to pounce on just the right moment to stop this contest.

Pobre Panzón. He was trying very hard not to cry but the tears kept pouring down his chubby cheeks. The day was hot, even for early September and even though it was still early afternoon. Panzón felt the sweat running down the back of his neck and the gravel poking the bottom of his feet through the thin soles of his shoes.

"*¿Quieres más?*" Forehead asked. He had his usual stupid, goat-like grin on his face.

"Hell, I haven't even felt it, bro'." Panzón was always game to the end. The truth was he was scared to death Forehead would do him serious harm. Maybe scramble his brains forever. But you couldn't show any fear. That was the code. Tears could stream down your face. That was O.K. as long as you didn't visibly and audibly sob.

"You wanna go another round, *ése?*"

"Let's get it on bro'. Why all the talk?"

Just as they were about to butt heads one more time Enrique, or Hank as he was called, came running down the back stairs of the school and he was shouting something.

"*Cálmense, ése.* Listen, I gotta tell you something."

"Stop! Contest over! Forehead, you win!" Augustín declared with a great flourish. Forehead always won, so there was no dishonor for anyone in this declaration. It didn't really matter if Hank had something important to say or not. For Augustín it was just a good excuse to stop the action.

Panzón pretended he was annoyed at the interruption of the contest. Although you could hardly call it a contest. Deep down, of course, Panzón was happy that something, anything, had stopped the merciless head butting.

"What's up, man?"

"Listen, Augustín. All you guys listen."

There was a hush as the gang formed a semi-circle around Forehead and Panzón. The gang included Hank, the biggest gossip, Adrián, who always smelled bad, Yes Yes who was called that because he said, "*sí, sí*", or "yes, yes" in English whenever he spoke. Forehead, Augustín, Panzón and Jefe, the oldest and toughest kid who was also always fair in settling fights, completed the gang. They turned their heads towards Hank.

"Media Luna is dead."

"You mean Mr. Rafael Luna?" asked Panzón.

"Who else could I mean, *pendejo*?" Hank said.

Augustín held his breath for a moment when he heard this. How could that be, he wondered to himself. Augustín had never really thought much about death and dying. He had lived in a world where everyone seemed to live forever. At least that's the way it was until last summer. That was when his father got this liver disease. And then his first cousin Lucas was murdered. It was hard to believe a year had gone by already. Since then his mother cried all the time. Especially because of what happened to Lucas.

"*Ayyyyy, cómo duele, m'hijo.*"

"Don't cry, Mamá. At least Lucas doesn't suffer no more."

"*Ayyyyy, m'hijo. Pero lo mataron tan malamente.* He was only seventeen years old and they shot him in the head." Then his mother would weep uncontrollably and Augustín's dad would try to calm her down. Finally Dr. Benavides gave her some pills and that seemed to stop the tears for a little while.

It all came back to Augustín now. How Lucas had borrowed his dad's '92 Sentra and had just bought a bag of fried chicken at Louie's Drive-In when an old '76 Pontiac had pulled up next to him and someone shot him in the head, instantly killing him.

"How did he die?" Augustín asked. His mind was still on Lucas but he knew he was asking about Media Luna.

"Well, the sonofabitch just up and died, *ése*."

"I won't shed no tears for him," Augustín said.

"*Tampoco*. He was mean. He used to beat the shit out of his wife. He made her black and blue all the time before she died," Jefe said.

Augustín remembered that it hadn't been that long ago, maybe two or three weeks earlier, when he and the gang had hidden behind the banks of the *acequia madre*, the main ditch or mother ditch, as it was called, and waited for Media Luna to come walking by on his way home from the paint factory on a Friday afternoon.

"*Aquí viene el viejo Luna*. Man he's drunk as a skunk," Augustín said.

"*Sí, sí*, here he comes stumbling and falling all over the place."

"Let's get him, man!" Panzón was always one to egg the gang on.

"Yeah, let's aim good at the old bastard," Jefe said.

"Media Luna, Media Luna, *aquí te viene una tuna!*" they shouted almost in unison.

Augustín remembered the hail of stones he and the others had unleashed against Mr. Luna. Everyone called him *media luna*, or "half-moon," because Mr. Luna was always "half lit", never quite sober. "*Borracho de aquellas*," or a well-known drunk, is the way everyone thought about Mr. Luna. Augustín could still see him stumbling and cursing and trying in vain to pick up stones to throw back at his attackers as they continued to taunt him with the *tunas* or "prickly pears" as they called the stones.

Augustín also remembered that sometimes the gang wasn't so lucky in its attacks on Media Luna. Once old man Luna had thrown a large stone that caught Panzón on his right cheekbone, just below the eye. Panzón had slumped to the ground without a sound, the right side of his face slightly caved-in. He had had surgery and it took months for him to recover. His parents had seen a lawyer but nothing came of it. If anything, Media Luna had become surlier. As soon as he recovered, Panzón was back with his buddies "making the rounds," as they said.

"So how did he die, *ése*? Jefe asked.

"Well, like I say, he just died. He was dead drunk. My dad said Mr. Luna had 'see roses of the liver," Hank said.

"Does that mean he saw roses before he died?" Adrián asked.

"Sounds like a neat way to die, *vato*. 'See roses' *y ay 'stuv*o. 'See roses' and good bye cruel world. *Chingao*," Panzón said. The gang always listened respectfully to the way Panzón talked about things.

"Maybe they call it 'see roses' to cover up an ugly way to die with a nice name," Jefe said.

"Ugh, I can just see a rotting liver *lleno de gusanos*. It smells bad and the worms crawl out and they come out through your ears and eyes and run down your nose like snot. Bullshit 'see roses'," Forehead said.

"Naa, I don't think it means nothing like what Jefe or Forehead say. I think it just means your liver gets real sick and then you die," Augustín said. "It's a disease. Cirrhosis. I can even spell it for you guys." Augustín spelled the word. As usual, everyone listened to Augustín because he did a lot of the thinking for the gang. He was always ready to propel them on to a new adventure.

"Shit. How do you know that, man?"

"My dad's got the disease," Augustín said. His dark brown eyes were hard when he said this and there was no hint of any emotion behind them. Augustín kept his feelings to himself. In fact, away from the gang he kept pretty much to himself. "Anyway guys, so what are we gonna do now?"

"Whaddaya mean what are we gonna do? Augustín, do you wanna go to Media Luna's funeral mass?" Jefe asked.

"No, I don't mean that. I mean, you know how we always wondered about old Media Luna's house? Like what was it really like inside?"

"Yeah."

"Now's our chance to take a good look inside." Augustín knew that the gang was not afraid to break into abandoned or boarded up houses. They had done that several times before and never got caught. They never took anything from these houses. Often they only succeeded in scaring themselves. But maybe this is why it was so much fun to be bad in this way.

"We've just got to wait a few days after the funeral. Media Luna's relatives are all from out of town and then they'll be gone."

"O.K. Augustín. Let's do it." With Jefe's backing, everybody nodded yes. Mr. Luna had died on Wednesday. The date for breaking into the old man's house was set for the following Monday.

II

Augustín had no idea what he hoped to find inside Media Luna's house. He thought about it for four long days as he fidgeted at home. The more he thought about Mr. Luna, the angrier he became about the old man. Media Luna had never liked kids. He was never friendly to anyone. He kept to himself and repaired car seat covers in his garage when he wasn't at the paint factory. The best anyone ever had to say about him was that at least he was happy and smiling when he was working on cars.

When Lucas had died Media Luna didn't even come by to say he was sorry. And that was another thing. One reason the days were so long waiting for Monday to arrive was because Augustín's parents, especially his mother, were still so fearful after what happened to Lucas, even though a year had passed. Augustín knew that his cousin Lucas was a Don Juan, a real lady's man, and that many a jealous boyfriend had made vague threats against "*El Lucas.*" Still, Lucas never really had trouble until he dated Emilia Manzanares. Emilia was also in high school and she was the same age as Lucas. She was Mexican, not Mexican-American. She had been born in the desert far south of Valle Vista. Although Emilia and her mother now lived on the United States side of the border, Emilia's aunt spent most of her time in Mexico where she gathered herbs and did who knows what. She didn't look like a gentle healer, a *curandera*, even though she claimed to be one. Rumor had it that she was a *bruja*, a witch, and a dangerous one at that. Everyone called her "*La Manzanares.*" Lucas, of course, hadn't taken any of this seriously. Neither had Augustín although he was curious about La Manzanares. He was fascinated by the contrast between La Manzanares with her dark clothes and somber face with deep set, heavily ringed eyes, and Emilia who had such an open smile and playful ways.

The kitchen door slammed and Augustín heard his mother carrying groceries. He went to help her.

"Thank you, *m'hijito*. I'm always so glad to find you here at home."

"Yes, I know." They put up the groceries and his mother began preparing for dinner.

"Mamá, do you remember Emilia?"

"Don't mention that name! Where did you hear it?"

"*Pues*, Mamá, all the kids knew her. We knew Lucas dated her and—"

"Don't say it! It isn't true that he broke her heart. She was going out with lots of guys. Not just Lucas."

"But Mamá—"

"Not another word!"

And with that Augustín lapsed into silence. He had intended to tell his mother that at the high school Emilia was always trying to push her home remedies, or remedios, for just about every ailment. The other students thought it was a little strange but they knew Emilia really believed in all that stuff and besides, she was so pretty and friendly.

St. Anthony's Elementary School was only two blocks away from the high school. Many of St. Anthony's more precocious students loved gossip and they knew everything that was going on at the high school. One day Augustín, then in the fourth grade, had seen Emilia's aunt suddenly come upon Lucas and Emilia when school let out.

"You better treat my niece right," he heard La Manzanares say.

"Or else?" Lucas asked in a teasing manner.

"Or else *you'll* be very sorry."

"Are you gonna put a spell on me or something?" Lucas laughed.

La Manzanares didn't reply but Augustín remembered the fierce cold look she gave Lucas. Augustín told the gang trouble was brewing for cousin Lucas.

Shortly after that, Lucas dropped Emilia. Dropped her cold. Emilia's mother begged him to come back to her daughter. Lucas simply shrugged it off. He started going out with other girls. And then he was murdered. Not long after that Emilia and her mother left Texas and returned to Mexico to live with family they had there.

During dinner, Augustín's mother regarded him with the large, luminous eyes of a frightened doe. He was sorry he had brought up the subject of Lucas earlier because now he knew it would be on her mind.

"It was so nice to find you here when I came home from the grocery store, *m'hijito*. When you are here I know—"

"—you are safe," Augustín finished for her. "Ay, Mamá, you can't worry about me twenty-four hours a day."

"Oh yes she can," his dad said.

"And you know that you worry, too. Look what happened to poor Lucas."

His dad rolled his eyes and said nothing.

"But Mom, that whole thing was weird. And besides, maybe Lucas had it com—." He bit his lips and plunged on. "I mean, Lucas was no angel."

"Augustín, how *dare* you criticize your dead cousin. He was a martyr! A saint!

"Yes, I know, Mamá."

"Your mouth should be washed out with strong soap!"

"I'm sorry, Mamá."

"If you're really sorry you'll wash the dishes and clean the stove."

"O.K., Mamá." Trapped again, he thought. His mother was very clever in trapping him into doing little duties around the house. Augustín sank into his dishwashing trance and tried to get through the job without thinking about how boring it was. He knew it had been a serious mistake to suggest that maybe Lucas had had it coming.

"Careful with those cups." His mother always barked orders at him when he washed the dishes.

"*Sí*, Mamá." He carefully set the cups on the upper shelf and continued thinking about what had happened to Lucas. He remembered he had just finished dinner with his mom and dad on a day like this one, a few weeks after Lucas had been buried. As usual, he was doing the dishes when he heard his parents speaking in strained tones.

"I've never seen a girl as angry as that Emilia."

"Ah, it's just women."

"Oh *sí*! What do you know about anything except booze?" His mother's deep hurt would often burst forth like this.

"That's right. I don't know anything." Under siege, his father would build a fortress of silence around himself.

"That's right. You're too stupid to see the obvious."

His father shrugged.

"*Va*! Don't you remember how Emilia's mother kept pestering your brother to tell Lucas to marry Emilia?"

"Hell yes I remember. And I remember my brother stuck by his son. He didn't try to tell Lucas what to do; ¡*Pues ya era hombre*! Aw, anyway I don't think Emilia was knocked up like her mother said."

"That's enough! How dare you use language like that with Augustín in the house? Don't you have any sense of dignity left?"

"Lay off me, woman."

"And then Emilia's aunt. That woman. La Manzanares." His mother plunged on. "Emilia and her mother dragged La Manzanares into it right away. That evil woman. That witch! I know she had something to do with murdering Lucas."

"Aw, nobody believes that witchcraft crap!"

"*You* don't believe. *I* don't believe. But *they* believe it! They still keep the old ways of Mexico! And that's why Lucas is dead!"

"You don't know that! You don't know anything!"

"I know more than you do! At least I'm sober!"

The predictable screaming ensued and then the lapse into silence like a truce that grew out of embarrassment. Augustín quietly finished drying the dishes.

Some time after the argument at home, Augustín remembered that Forehead had seen La Manzanares on the banks of the Rio Grande, just south of the oldest neighborhood of Valle Vista. Forehead said she and Media Luna "were really talking up a storm." Then Media Luna had given her something and La Manzanares put it in a paper bag. She tied the bag and threw it into the river and both she and Media Luna quickly left by separate paths. The river was shallow here and Forehead had jumped into it a few moments later and had rescued the bag before it could sink. It contained chicken feathers, the arrow-shaped hood ornament of an old Pontiac, pig guts, a small black plastic ball with a saint painted on it, and tiny eyes like those of a mouse or a rat and all kinds of other terrible things. At least that's what Forehead said. Forehead's dad had called the police about the bag, but they couldn't prove anything by it. The police did suspect, however, that Emilia's mother and La Manzanares had hired a hit man but they couldn't ever prove it.

"Augustín!" his mother shrieked. "Since when do the dishes go on the bottom shelf?"

"Sorry, Mamá." Augustín wanted to talk to his mother about the bag in the river, but he was afraid it would only trigger a family quarrel. Sometimes silence seemed best.

"And when you finish, you better read. You better learn something besides running around with your little gang if you're ever going to amount to anything."

"*Sí*, Mamá." He hated to read. Actually, when he thought about it, he realized reading was the easiest thing for him to do. But he found the school books boring. They had nothing to do with his life, his family, his neighborhood. The stories he read in school seemed to be about people from another planet. Boring people. From a boring planet. He was glad that it was Sunday night and that tomorrow was a school day. No more dreary quarrels and even drearier silences at home. And he would anxiously wait all day for the last class to end so that he and the gang could get on with what was for them their real and secret life. Then something interesting would happen. Tomorrow was the big day.

III

The yellow school busses were all lined up across from the school yard and St. Anthony's students marched on board like little soldiers. Nearby, many parents were parked and waiting to pick up their children.

Augustín and the gang lived easy walking distance from the school, only a couple of blocks away. They had already told their parents that they were going to play "down by the ditch" for a while before coming home.

The ditch was the *acequia madre* that carried the river water to the smaller irrigation ditches and then to the fields during the spring and early summer. By autumn, the ditch was dry and a tangle of weeds and grasses grew along its banks. So the parents didn't mind their kids playing along the ditch as long as there were several of them together.

The gang quietly slipped around the other children and left St. Anthony's like skilled commandos. Within minutes they cut across two empty lots and were over the ditch banks and hidden from general view. They moved north along the ditch bottom. Before long they were peering over the ditch bank at the back side of Media Luna's boarded up house and the driveway winding away from it.

To Augustín the back side looked ominous. It formed a long room, probably a garage of some sort, with no windows whatsoever. A rusted white sign with green letters that said "SEAT COVERS" in large capital letters rested against the back wall. Next to the long room was a smaller room with a boarded up window. Augustín knew that Media Luna's home was built in a U shape, but with a very wide bottom. The gang was now observing this long back side of the home from their hiding places on the *acequia madre*. The south side of the U was flanked by a small ditch running off the *acequia madre*. On the north, an apple orchard offered excellent cover to small bodies.

"*Mira, vatos,*" Jefe said. "Forehead, you, Panzón, Adrián, and Yes Yes move up the little ditch we just crossed and check out that side of the house."

"I don't want to go with Forehead," Panzón said.

"It don't make no difference, *vato*. Go with him! We have to stick together or this whole thing might not work."

"*Bueno,*" was all Panzón said. The boys knew the dangers were real. There was always the possibility of the cops cruising by and catching them inside the house. Or a stranger might drive by, see them, and call the cops. Worse still, one of their parents might drive by and wonder what the boys were doing at Mr. Luna's home. The sense of danger made them draw close.

"Augustín, Hank and me will move up through the orchard. We'll meet at the big cottonwood in Media Luna's front yard," Jefe said.

The cottonwood offered very little cover from the house but that didn't matter since the house was empty. If a car came speeding by on North River Road the boys could always pretend they were just playing around the cottonwood and not interested in the house at all.

Once they had reached the cottonwood, the gang surveyed Media Luna's home.

"You know, it's kind of creepy," Augustín said.

"Whaddaya mean? It's always creepy doing this."

"No, this is creepy in a special way. We called him Media Luna," Augustín continued, "and his house is in the shape of a *media luna*, a half-moon shape. That's creepy."

From the cottonwood, in fact, the boys were looking right down the open end of the patio partially enclosed by the three inner walls of Mr. Luna's home. Unlike many similar homes, Media Luna's patio was not attractive. It lacked a porch and the inner walls were bare. There were few windows on the northern wing of the house and only one exterior door facing the patio. Instinctively they knew the patio was a potential trap to be avoided.

"All the outside windows on the left side are boarded up, *sí, sí.*"

"You mean the north side." Jefe liked military precision.

"Same thing on the south side," Hank said. "But Jefe or Forehead could knock out the boards on the first room on the right. They don't look that strong."

"I'll do it," Forehead said.

"Panzón, you stay here at the tree when we go in. Whistle loud if anyone comes. You say that you were just playing here alone."

"O.K. Jefe." Panzón could not run very fast and so he was always chosen to stand guard and delay potential pursuers. Besides, he looked so innocent adults usually believed anything he said.

"Remember," Augustín said, "if we hear Panzón whistle, then we all split the way we came, through the orchard and along the ditches." With the exception of Panzón, the boys were fast and they were confident that they could escape almost anyone through the maze of ditches, gardens and orchards along North River Road near the Rio Grande.

"Well, are we going to do it?" Forehead was always anxious for action.

"Let's go," Augustín said.

"Go, go, go!" Jefe said.

IV

Forehead bounded towards the outside window of the first room on the north wing. When he got there, Augustín, Hank and Jefe followed. Just like they had seen in countless war movies. Within seconds Forehead had the boards down and a window pane removed without breaking it. In less than a minute the door facing the patio flew open. Adrián and Yes Yes quickly ran inside, leaving Panzón alone at the cottonwood.

Once inside the boys looked cautiously around in what had to be the living room. White sheets covered the obvious shapes of chairs and a couch. The stale air was thick with dust and the lingering smell of beer and whiskey bottles.

"Just like in ghost stories," Augustín mused to himself. The boys moved into the next room, a simple bedroom with a single bed and two chairs. In the inside corner, facing the patio, was a small bathroom with a toilet and shower stall. Dead cockroaches, about six of them, were belly up around the base of the toilet. Straight back from the bedroom was a third small room, the kitchen. It had a very old refrigerator, the kind that stood on four legs, and an equally old gas stove that stood on four short curved legs. Otherwise the kitchen was bare and uninteresting.

"*A la v* —! Look what's in here," Forehead said. He had just found the light switch for the long room near the door leading into it. Now he was peering into this room that formed the bottom of the U.

All the boys piled into the long room. The light bulb was very dim but it was obvious that this was Media Luna's work space. There was a clutter of empty and half-empty paint cans along the inner wall. There were step ladders and tools of all kinds against the outer wall. Piles of newspapers, large plastic sheets and automobile parts littered the space. Empty beer cans and whisky bottles were everywhere. Near the door leading into the next wing of the house was a neat row of small metal waste cans. They were filled with empty liquor bottles. Everything was covered with a fine layer of dust.

Augustín looked around and then something caught his attention. There was an uneven pile of five or six automobile hoods leaning topsy turvy against the outer wall, near the garage door that led to the driveway outside. And there it was, almost in the middle of the pile. The nightmare of his cousin Lucas came back to him when he recognized the shape of an old 70's Pontiac hood. It had a grey base coat as if it were being prepared for a new paint job. But it wasn't the color that caught Augustín's attention. It was the missing hood ornament. The base coat had been applied *before* the hood ornament had been removed, as if in great haste. Augustín knew this because the rust-covered metal where the ornament had been was outlined by the ghost of the Pontiac hood ornament. The shape was that of a shield and for some reason Augustín remembered stories he had read about medieval knights who wandered around trying to right the wrongs of the world. Augustín remembered Forehead's story about the Pontiac ornament in the paper sack. Of course, he reasoned, none of this proved anything. But it made him feel very uneasy.

"Hey man, come over here and look at this!" Forehead motioned to Augustín to cross the room and take a closer look at the waste baskets filled with the empty bottles.

"Well, what about them.?

"*Ándale*, Augustín, you're so smart. Take a close look at the bottles."

At first Augustín only saw empty bottles. But then he noticed that the waste baskets furthest from the door were the older ones. They contained mostly whiskey bottles, half pints, and they were very cheap brands. "Heavenly Daze." "Southern Fire." "Mountain Hawk." Brands like that. In the newest waste basket, the one nearest the door, the brands were the expensive ones. Augustín had heard his dad speak of "Wild Horses" and "Gentleman Jim" in tones of reverence. "The rich know how to live well," his dad would say.

"Media Luna must have been making a few bucks in his last days," Forehead said.

"Yup," Augustín said. "It looks like all of a sudden Media Luna came into some money."

"Like maybe the bastard did some kind of job for somebody?"

"Like maybe this was a good place to chop stolen cars and who knows what else went on here. You're getting pretty sharp, Forehead. Next time we plan a job, you better help us out, *ése*."

Forehead could hardly contain the pride Augustín's remark gave him.

"Let's see what's back here," Jefe said. He was the first into the next room that formed the beginning of the south side of the house. It had a small band saw, a couple of work benches and more automobile parts—seats, fenders, bumpers—stacked and scattered around.

"Let's get to the last room," Hank said. The urgency in his voice was shared silently by each boy. With every passing moment, the risks of staying inside the house grew larger and larger inside their minds.

"Wow!"

"*¡Mira no más!*"

"Yeah, just look! Hey man, I don't like this." There was a slight quiver in Adrián's voice.

The heavy oppressiveness of the room descended on Augustín the moment he entered it. Each of the four walls of the last room had pictures pasted up. Hundreds of them altogether. They were mostly in color and for the most part they had been cut out of mystery magazines. Each picture had its own gruesome scene. A hanging here, a dead man with a bullet hole through his head there, and blood and gore in every picture.

In the center of the room was a beautiful, expensive looking mahogany coffee table, the kind you see in pictures of rich people's homes. But this coffee table had a butcher knife stabbed right down into the middle of it.

"Man, let's get out of here!" Hank didn't even try to hide how nervous he was.

"Hey, this guy was really sick, man. *¡Híjole!*," Jefe said.

Augustín just stood there at first but then he slowly began to look around and carefully register every object in the room. He noticed a cheap chest of drawers and he went to it. He carefully opened the first drawer. There was a rat's nest of small objects—paper clips, old eyeglasses, newspaper cuttings, matches, cigarette holders, an old deck of cards, ancient sticks of gum, things like that—inside the first drawer. In the corner of the drawer Augustín noticed the small stack of pictures of women. What everyone called dirty pictures. The kind of pictures he was curious about but that made him blush when one of his buddies would bring a picture like that to school.

He closed the top drawer and opened the next lower one. It also contained a variety of small objects. Among them were what looked like six or seven round black balls. When Augustín looked closer, he saw that they were not balls at all. They were gear shift knobs. The kind that you could still see on some trucks and on very old cars. But these were very unusual gear shift knobs. The top side of each knob, where the palm of the hand would normally rest, had a bright painting of a saint or of the Virgin Mary embedded in clear plastic. Augustín remembered that when a distant relative of his had driven up from Mexico he had had a religious gear shift knob like this. The moment he realized what he was looking at, Augustín rushed over to Forehead.

"Forehead, remember when you found that paper sack filled with all that *bruja* stuff?"

"Yeah, it was witch stuff all right."

"Yeah, but didn't you say you found a black ball inside the sack?"

"Yeah. There was a little plastic ball. It looked kind of black, I guess. I ain't sure though, you know, with all the pig guts and everything."

"Did it have a holy painting like this?"

Forehead's eyes almost popped out of his head when Augustín showed him the gear shift knob. "Hey, that's just like it! I almost forgot."

"Oh man, let's get out of here." Adrián was about to panic.

"Calm down", Augustín said. He thought he had to imitate Jefe and show no fear. He could control the impulse to run for a moment or two but many things passed through his head in those few seconds. He could feel it in his bones for sure that Media Luna had something to do with Lucas's murder. But just what he didn't know. Probably would never know. What got to him most were the pictures on the walls. They weighed down on him like everything that was ugly and heavy in the adult world, like his dad drinking, like his mom nagging, like his own ignorance about almost everything. His mouth was dry and it became hard for him to breathe. He remembered the catechism and the bible stories the nuns at school recited and he thought he must be feeling the weight of fallen angels.

At that moment a crow cawed outside. It wasn't Panzón's shrill whistle but it might as well have been. For one instant the boys glanced at each other and their eyes said flee right now, get out of this house, quickly. "We're out of here!" Jefe bellowed.

There was no way they would retrace their steps back through Media Luna's house. All thought became reflex now. They kicked open the boarded up window and this time they weren't careful about the window panes. One by one they quickly cleared the broken shards of glass and ran down the south wall of the house towards the *acequia madre*. Like good soldiers, Jefe and Augustín waited for everyone else to clear the window and then they fled. By then Panzón had noticed what was going on and slow though he was, he, too, was half way to the *acequia madre*.

Autumn's sharp air, the clean blue sky, the openness of the land and the shimmering light of the sun along the poplars and cottonwoods lining the banks of the Rio Grande dispelled the darkness of Media Luna's house. As Augustín ran, that house seemed to fade into a dimly remembered past. He couldn't solve the problem of cousin Lucas's death but there were enough clues back there to something that had happened. Adults would solve it. Or maybe they wouldn't. He knew he couldn't and that it didn't matter because Media Luna was dead and nothing could help cousin Lucas now. Augustín was running hard and images of his father and mother swirling in a mist of alcohol and harsh words flickered in his mind. He wanted to be rid of these images, to be free forever. At the same time, he wanted somehow to understand his own world, to learn everything about it and also about the wider world beyond the mountains and rivers that formed the horizons of his childhood. And suddenly the gang seemed very small and he knew that his days in it were numbered and that he would miss it and that he had no choice although he didn't know exactly why things had to be this way. He sucked in huge mouthfuls of air and his feet became swift and light as he ran.

The Rare Capture & Transformation of Canyon to Body by Fog

Jefferson Adams

>*There are beasts so large that it's hard
>to know they exist until you find that
>you live insideof them.*

There was fog so thick in the canyon
That the land surrendered its edge
And a white-fleet of vapor
Took over, ridge to ridge

And down the rocks to the river
And in between where the pinon

And scrub oak threw their shadows
To the sky, all of the shadows
Gone white in the shock;
The sky, too, gone white.

"It is this day," I said to myself
"This day alone erases the earth."

To see a whole landscape erased
To be yourself erased by fog

Is like walking into God's hands:
All sense lifted right out of you
So your own hands no longer shake
And there is nothing to misjudge.

The tears overwhelming your eyes
Allow no color, no distance
No scent—what sound stumbles
Through to your ears seems
Savagely muted, bruised;
Everything lost to the intense

Fragility of a thing both greater
And less than itself: a lake
Or small ocean held in air
And close, like a kiss—everything
Quiet, pressed, locked down.

Everything dangerous covered.

Three Mornings In The Floating World

Jeanne Shannon

I

I was twelve that summer at Chichén Itzá, when a feathery
priest threw me down a well, saying I was the maiden the
rain gods required. You hid in the almond grove and wept;
you had wanted to marry me.

The priest told me that after death I would marry the sun.
I had wanted to marry you.

I sank down through the whorled water, black-green; through
the jade and the beaten gold. When dark fell, my drowned
eyes turned to emeralds. I gazed up at the citron stars.

At dawn, thin nails of rain fell slantingly through the
parched air. Transparent rain, piercing the parchment light
over the grain fields. Corncrakes flew up, foretelling
harvests. The gods were pleased.

You walked through the rainy groves and whispered my name.
I watched you with my emerald eyes.

II

I met you at Uxmal, three lifetimes later. You were married
to someone else.

And one morning in Riobamba, you were selling live chickens
in the marketplace. You sold me a rooster. I never told
you my name. I was married to someone else.

III

I never saw you again, until that morning last April, north
of Santa Fe. Your eyes were blue, the blue fire of wild chicory.

You led me into a luminous cavern. Cannas and starflowers
bloomed at the entrance. You gave me a silver turtle
with eyes made of emeralds. It came alive when you touched
it.

You took me away with you. You piloted a speedboat through
teal-green sea waves. We sailed faster and faster until we
were flying. The sea fell away beneath us. You guided the
boat among lemony stars; we grazed the orbits of purple
planets.

We flew over Uxmal and Riobamba. It was October at Chichén
Itzá. Corncrakes flew up from the fields; I thought for a
moment I saw a well.

But, oh, the lemony stars were flowering, and planets were
succulent as grapes.

In Orion, cannas were blooming in the yards. Turtles
crawled over floors made of malachite.

North of Perseus, dark owls were calling.

Black Widow

Sharon Hatfield

When Cecilita was five her cousins Roberto y Rafael, devils like their father Armando, enticed her into the tool shed with a Tootsie Roll and pulled down her underwear and inserted a stick into her secret place.

They did this when it became obvious they would not be able to insert their own wormish, immature organs into her. Their lack of ability to accomplish what their elders did with such ease and gusto left them angry, brutish.

The stick was long and had sharp twigs on it, and even a few elm seedlings in their pale green casings found their way inside her. Afterward, she knelt beside the shack and vomited. She was sore for *dias ocho*. Knowing already the futility of protest, she told no one. She was ashamed and worried that it was somehow her fault.

The aura of furtive sex was lively in the three-room shack where she lived with her mother, two sisters, a brother, two aunts, two uncles, eleven cousins and her abuela. The shack was long and narrow, with a dirt floor and spaces between the boards of the walls. The spaces were covered with newspapers but the evil eternal wind ripped them, letting in thick red dirt in the springtime and cold air in the winter. Her mother and aunts patched them endlessly with flour and water. Cecilita looked at the strange designs on the paper and wondered what they meant.

They belonged to a world of which she was dimly but vitally aware: the gringo world of the men for whom her family worked, the men who drove large tractors and shining Ford pickups. She saw white girls of her own age, dressed in ruffled pink dresses, get into great yellow school buses in the mornings and come back in the afternoon, laughing and running so that their ponytails swished back and forth behind them. When she would stare at them too long her mother would poke her with a long finger, and Cecilita would return to her work.

She slept between her two sisters, wrapped summer and winter in a cocoon of thin green blanket that covered her face to keep the mice and cockroaches from her. Nothing could keep out the sounds of the large tired family—snorting, snoring, shrieking, moaning, belching, farting, sighing, crying, and worst of all, laboring women giving birth. At these times, her aunts and cousins seemed more like the cows in the field than humans to Cecilita, who was ashamed of these thoughts.

At an early age she noticed the smells, the rustlings, the slitherings of bare brown feet that led to the new babies. In order to sleep she put her fingers into her ears, lulling herself with repetition of simple words she liked the sound of—mesquite, *pequeño, moreno*, but sometimes *malo, malo, malo*, again and again.

When she was seven, Roberto y Rafael were successful in trapping her in the outhouse and affirming their manhood. She bled, and wiped slowly with the pages of a Sears catalog. Her hair stuck to her head, wet with the July heat, but only sweat rolled down her cheeks. She would not cry, but her sister Isella watched her come slowly from the outhouse and told their sister Esmerelda, who told their mother Maria.

Maria did not care. It was just the way things were, she told Cecilita firmly that night, and she would get used to it soon enough. Her black eyes held a secret Cecilita couldn't decipher, and a small gentleness crept into her thick fingers as they skimmed over Cecilita's face. She spoke in a low voice. The men worked hard in the fields all day and were tired. They were angry at the gringos and their hard lives and somehow the lunging and spurting made them feel better. Women were the holders, the keepers, the containers of everything in the world, Maria said. Without women everything would squirt everywhere and the world would be a mess and everyone would drown. It was good to be a woman and not a man.

Cecilita wondered how it made the women feel, who also worked all day in the fields and then cooked and cared for *los hijos* as well. She did not ask, for she knew her own mother was often underneath her uncle the devil Armando. Esmerelda told her it was like paying rent, for *el padre* was dead and they had no place else to go. Isella said it was like in the Bible, when a man married the widow of his brother.

When she was nine, her uncle began slipping into bed with her sisters. Cecilita would waken to find the mattress jiggling beside her. She lay as still as death, hardly breathing. All the anger in the world seemed to collect inside her head, until she thought it would crack open and let out all the things that would drown them.

Her sisters didn't seem to mind, and Maria was grateful to be left alone to sleep. Cecilita let go of the love she had held for them.

When she was eleven, Armando began eying her long legs. Esmerelda distracted him with her own, and Cecilita let herself care for her sister again, but she began to sleep outside, even in the cold, and would rage and scream if they tried to force her inside. She bound her breasts with a long rag and plucked pubic hairs as they sprouted. When her blood came she chopped at her long black hair with a knife. She never smiled.

She refused to bathe, and stopped speaking. Sometimes she growled. New words formed inside her, new worlds. Old women came and spoke to her of plants and buttons and lizards; her *abuela* called her *loco* and patted her head sorrowfully. Late one night, when everyone else was asleep, the old woman crept through the darkness to Cecilita and tried to baptise her in the stock tank, fearing demons and damnation, but Cecilita rose from the scummy cold water with a fierce anger, a freed tongue. She cursed her *abuela*, fearing neither devils nor men. She walked off into the night. No one followed her. She didn't look back.

At dawn she came to a small town and rested in front of a gas station. She went behind it and slept to forget her hunger. When she woke a *gringo* with green eyes was smiling at her. His hair was blond and fluttered like angel wings. He held out to her a bag of Doritos and a Dr. Pepper.

A wild spring wind began to blow, and all the seeds of the world were blowing in that wind, she knew, dandelions and tumbleweeds, loco weeds and bumblebee babies. She looked into the eyes of the man and was filled with the knowledge, at last, of the power women had, the advantage of being female. Slowly she took the food.

Later, after the *gringo* had done what men do and was sleeping, she took a long thin knife from his kitchen and slipped it neatly into his chest. She took the money from his wallet and lay down to sleep away the heat of the afternoon. As the sun began to set, flaming like a great ball, she rose, smoothed her skirt and stepped outside. Stars were like holes in the sky, the air was cool on her hot skin. When it was completely dark she started walking down the road toward the next town.

FOR JOAN

Robert Edwards

Somewhere, under the painted metals of the sky,
there are mountains the color of blue cornmeal,
and sand fine as masa under the feet
of Navajo women spooning pinto beans over frybread
or drizzling sopapillas with mesquite honey.

Outside your northern window,
winter grinds quartz against the abstract sun.
But there is a peppery heat in your kitchen,
gentle generosities mixed in the border sauces,
soups that illuminate the spine, tamale rituals,
salsas and quesadillas that make us remember
to shake out our shoes in the morning.
Slap, slap goes the tortilla from hand to hand.
From your oven comes a cuisine,
neither native nor foreign,
spiced with the crazy, poor, good old times . . .

A landscape dangerous with corn, with anger
beneath the patience, and poverty, like dust,
over everything. We have all travelled
so far from where we made our first last stand,
where we were legendary and young and found
the friends we'll always believe in.
But there is money here, warm houses and jobs,
a way to continue the beautiful, useless things
stolen from sleep and rent.
We all return, carrying what changed us:
accents, recipes, defeats, the first laughter
that said our fathers might be wrong.

Tired teacher, correcting student papers
by lamplight, you've given up so much, and now
horses are standing in Chaco Canyon,
looking over their twitching flanks at the moon
descending cedar ladders into abandoned kivas.

A transparent silence settles like glass snow . . .

There is still so much to leave behind.
Outside, among the sirens, the night is as cold
as you remember it, but the old wool blanket,
sprinkled with red dust,
that you pull against your cheek,
smells like home.

Old Oraibi

Robert Edwards

1.

Squash blossom, bean sprout, gourd—
a singing to the seed
of the October sun of old Oraibi,[1]
forbidden once to *pahaanas*[2]
because tourists looted
planted prayer-sticks for souvenirs,
were rude and trampled cornmeal into sand.

Hard times are history here,
and legend of blackened scars on rock
where lightning struck the corn
growing between potsherds from jars
that carried water to thirsty conquistadors—
smashed when free lips sang again.

And it is because we have so much future
and so little past
that we would study endurance in the face
of an old man lifting a ladle of water to his lips.

A laughing boy leaps an adobe wall,
and a woman selling bullroarers
bids us see what we would see,
but to touch nothing, to take
no photographs, and to behave
as guests of the living and the dead.

---

[1] Dating from the 1100s A.D., Old Oraibi is believed by many to be the oldest continuously occupied settlement in North America.

[2] Hopi word for white people

2.

At the Mesa's edge is an old church,
the rubble of its boards and stones
a sieve for the true names of the wind.
Its Christian cisterns are empty,
except for a bull snake coiled in a sink of shadow.

Recent heavens found no root here.
What remains is Hisatsinom[3] earth,
a dry stew of potsherds broken
in a trail back to first water.
Rocks or ruins dark against the bright distance:
foundations we would follow to claim
the ceremony and labor of hope for our own.

3.

Out of respect we take no more than memory
and the windblown dust we breathe.

       Though we, too, want to climb
a ladder leaned against the sky,
through the sipapu[4], into fields of tall corn,
into a green fifth world,

embracing all the lost brothers and sisters,
all the scattered tribes gathered home at last.

---

[3] Hopi name for themselves

[4] Hopi word for "Place of Emergence." The Hopi believe that there have been three previous worlds below the one we know, which is the fourth world. With the collapse of each successive world, humans climbed to the sky, frequently with animal assistance, and emerged through a hole or *sipapu*, into a new and better world.

Doña Fortunata and Andrés
Cookies, Cuentos and Friendship

Mary Helen Fierro Klare

Doña Fortunata took a steaming tray of brown sugar cookies out of the oven. Their delicate cinnamon smell spread quickly to every corner of the small kitchen.

"Delicious *canela* cookies to offer the children after *los cuentos*," she told herself, brushing a few wisps of gray hair from her wrinkled forehead. Her face was flushed a rosy pink from the oven heat which had also steamed up the lenses of her metal frame glasses. She grabbed the tip of her flour-stained apron and wiped her glasses, then slowly and carefully, lowered herself into one of her old kitchen chairs. Doña Fortunata thought that baking cookies was not an easy task for someone of her advanced age to perform. *¡Mucho trabajo!* However, she knew how much the children would enjoy the cookies with chocolate milk after the story telling.

Being somewhat of the village storyteller, a distinction she fully enjoyed, Doña Fortunata took pleasure in telling her stories to the neighborhood children during the summer months. The cool, northern New Mexico evenings in the little town of Aurora were ideal for sitting outside in her garden, where they would be surrounded by roses, geraniums, daisies, hollyhocks and a star-studded dark blue sky. It was the perfect setting for the unfolding of her tales, legends and myths—most of which she had learned from her mother, who in turn had learned from *her* mother, and some of which Doña Fortunata had created herself. Her young, captive audience would sit, enthralled for hours, listening to her melodious voice spinning its magic as she knitted, her needles fluttering up and down soundlessly like butterfly's wings, in a steady rhythm that softly punctuated her words. Sometimes Doña Fortunata wondered if the children felt the same way she had when she had been a little girl sitting at her mother's feet listening to her musical voice telling stories for hours on end. They had been fantastic stories too! *Cuentos* that had filled her head with magic and *sueños*, dreams that floated in her head for days at a time.

Sitting quietly in her antiquated kitchen, Doña Fortunata's thoughts turned to the most eager and attentive listener among the children—Andrés. He also happened to be her favorite. She wondered why he hadn't been coming around lately. Sometimes, in the process of telling a story, she would catch a glimpse of Andrés's large brown eyes and notice the dream-like expression in them. Doña Fortunata could tell by his faraway look that his vivid imagination had taken him a thousand miles away. She knew that Andrés was not just simply listening to her story with all his heart but he was living every moment of it as well.

Doña Fortunata smiled at the thought of Andrés. *"Qué niño tan bueno,"* she said to herself. "A sweet boy . . . *y muy vivo también! Sí,* Andrés is a very smart *niño.*"

As she was thinking about Andrés, she heard a soft knock at the front door followed by the sound of a familiar husky voice calling out tunefully, "Doña Fortu-naaa-taaaa."

With a happy smile on her face, the *anciana* walked as quickly as she could manage from the kitchen, through the neat living room with its many lace doilies, to the front door.

"Andrés! *¡Pasa! ¡Qué sorpresa!* What a surprise!," she said, opening the door for him.

"Hello, Doña Fortunata", said Andrés, quietly.

"Andrés! I am so happy to see you," said Doña Fortunata cheerfully. *"¿Cómo has estado?"*

"Oh . . . fine," he said shrugging his shoulders. He couldn't help noticing the sweet smell of freshly baked cookies in the air. It made the inside of his stomach feel warm—the best it had felt in days. He even felt a little hungry.

"Vamos a la cocina," she said, motioning toward the kitchen.

"Follow me, I baked your favorite kind of *galletitas* today." Doña Fortunata noticed that Andrés looked preoccupied.

"Oh . . . I'm not very hungry," said Andrés, eying the tall platter of delicious looking cinnamon cookies on the tile counter.

"*Cómo que* 'I'm not hungry'?" she asked frowning. This was not the Andrés she knew. That exuberant, animated boy who would frequently visit her after school— usually ravenous—with a head full of *historias* to tell her about his day.

"Andrés, have at least one cinnamon *galletita,* with a glass of milk," she urged.

"Well . . . maybe," Andrés said, weakening. "I can't stay long today Doña Fortunata. My Mama wants me home as soon as possible. She says we have a lot of work to do around the house . . . especially around the yard." His voice dropped as he voiced the last words.

"¿Qué pasa? What is the matter?" asked Doña Fortunata. *"Cuéntame."*

Not waiting for an answer from him, she put four round cookies on a small plate that had a purple grape pattern on it. She then opened her old-fashioned refrigerator and slowly poured Andrés a tall glass of milk.

"You look *muy triste*, Andrés...too sad," she said, glancing worriedly at him. "Tell me what is bothering you."

Andrés remained lost in his thoughts. He knew something did not feel right in his world. But he didn't know exactly what was wrong.

He pulled out a chair to sit on, and glanced at the old woman moving slowly around the narrow kitchen. Because both his parents worked, Andrés often stopped at Doña Fortunata's after school for a visit. Sometimes she would try one of her new stories on him. He always enjoyed this. It was like getting a preview of an upcoming event. Even though he thought she had to be at least a hundred years old—or even more than that—he considered her to be his special friend. She was always interested in anything he had to say. No matter what it might be. Doña Fortunata was never too busy to listen to him. She never told him to hurry up saying what he had to say so she could get on with her work. Even his best friend Leo was sometimes not a very good listener. In fact, Leo always wanted to do the talking and have Andrés do all the listening. Knowing the way girls never stopped chattering at school, Andrés thought maybe Leo, who had five sisters, never got a chance to talk at home.

Doña Fortunata sat herself at the small wooden kitchen table across from Andrés. Neither spoke. The old lady knitted and the boy took small half-hearted bites out of his warm cookie. Outside the kitchen window they could hear a little bird singing melodiously in the herb garden. Had they looked out the window, they would have seen a pair of hummingbirds fighting for the best spot on the red feeder hanging from one of the piñon trees.

Doña Fortunata studied Andrés' sad face. The light is missing from his usually bright eyes, she thought.

"Doña Fortunata, why didn't you ever get married?" blurted Andrés. "My Mama says you're lucky you never married."

Doña Fortunata had long since stopped feeling defensive when asked this question. She was too old to feel sensitive about never having married. *No le importa a nadie,* she thought. It is nobody's business. Nevertheless, she was startled to be asked this by Andrés.

"Ten year old boys shouldn't be asking old women such questions," she said.

Andrés stole a quick look at her face. He couldn't tell by the tone of her voice whether or not he had made her angry.

"Never mind why I never married," Doña Fortunata continued. "Your *Mamá* is lucky she found a good *esposo* such as your father . . . Ray is a good man, and she should consider herself even more lucky to have a good boy like you for a son."

"Oh . . . I don't think she feels lucky she has me," said Andrés softly, returning a half eaten cookie back to his plate.

"*¿Que dices Andrés?* What are you saying? Of course she feels lucky to have you for her *hijito*. She loves you very much."

"I miss my Papa," Andrés said suddenly. "He went away two weeks ago and hasn't come back. When I ask my Mama when he will be back, she gets sad, and says we'll have to wait and see."

Doña Fortunata, pensive, knitted quietly as she listened to Andrés. She let him go on speaking without interrupting. Except for the bird's singing in the garden, it was very quiet and still outside. Occasionally the fragrant cinnamon warmth inside the tiny kitchen would be cooled by a fresh, light breeze making its way through the counter window. It gently ruffled the yellowed lace curtains.

"I think maybe my Papa left because of something I did. Maybe I shouldn't have nagged him so much about getting me a pony. He kept telling me we couldn't afford it. But I kept asking for one. I think he got tired of me."

"No, no, no!" said Doña Fortunata quickly. "Your father loves you, he would never get tired of you." But under her breath Doña Fortunata talked to herself. *"Qué lástima,* what a shame. Such a nice *familia.* I hope it's nothing serious. I must speak to Ana soon. Andrés is hurting too much."

"I think my Mama misses him as much as I do because she cries a lot. She tries to hide it from me. But she can't fool me. Sometimes I hear her crying softly in her room at night."

"Ay, pobrecita tu Mamá. Of course she must be suffering too. *Y pobre de ti.* And what of your Papá?" Doña Fortunata spoke to no one in particular as she voiced her thoughts out loud.

"Drink your milk and eat your cookies Andresito," she said kindly. "Everything is going to be all right. *No te apures.* Don't you worry. *Dios es muy grande."*

Having expressed his thoughts—thoughts that had been bothering him for many days—to his kind and elderly friend, Andrés felt a little better about himself and everything in general. He sure missed his Papa though. They were special buddies. He missed the fun they always had playing games and especially missed the hikes they took on weekends. His Papa just had to come home soon, thought Andrés. They all loved each other too much for this not to happen. Maybe then his Mama would laugh again. Once his Papa was back, surely everything would be as before.

Feeling hopeful about his future, Andrés' thoughts turned to story-telling.

"Doña Fortunata, the other day I asked my Mama why she couldn't make up stories the way you can."

"And what did she tell you?" asked Doña Fortunata, a little absentmindedly. Her thoughts were still on Andrés' family.

"Mama said, she's too busy taking care of me and my father, and too busy with her job to make stories up. She says she doesn't have that kind of time."

"Dice bien tu Mama. She is right, of course. Your mother has too many responsibilities. *Y mucho en que pensar,* too much to think about. There is no room in her head for making up stories."

"Do you know what I think Doña Fortunata?"

"No . . . what do you think Andrés?"

As she continued to knit, the *anciana* wondered if money had been at the root of the problem with Andrés' family. No one in this poor mountain village had money to spare. Most of the men and some of the women worked in the city, earning enough money to live a good but simple life in their little *pueblito* of Aurora. Yet everyone appeared to be happy;,always friendly and neighborly, going about their business from day to day.

"Dime . . . what do you think?" Doña Fortunata asked a second time, never raising her eyes from her knitting.

Andrés wrinkled his smooth tanned brow a little as he tried to formulate his thoughts. Then he spoke quickly.

"I think that your stories are your children."

"O, sí?"

"Yes. You have many of them— and you have favorites. Just like my friend Leo says his mother has. Leo says his oldest and his youngest sisters are his mother's favorite children."

Doña Fortunata smiled at this comment. She knew that Leo had his own special view of the world. She stopped knitting for a moment and looked at Andrés.

"Sí, it's true I have favorites," she said, smiling.

Encouraged by her answer, Andrés continued.

"You take care of them—your stories, I mean—like children. You make sure you never forget them and you try to improve them and make them better. You can't ever be lonely Doña Fortunata, because your stories are always with you, living in your head."

Doña Fortunata smiled again, this time a little wistfully.

"You're a sweet boy, Andrés. *Eres muy buen niño.* Help yourself to more cookies and milk." Doña Fortunata's dark eyes glowed gently with affection behind the round frames of her glasses as she watched Andrés leave the table and walk over to the refrigerator to pour himself more milk. With her kind face lost in faraway thoughts, Doña Fortunata went back to her knitting.

The warm, white light of the afternoon sun poured into the kitchen through the square window, giving everything in the tiny crowded room a soft, faded texture. A mixture of floral fragrances from the large multi-colored garden penetrated the front screen door, and made their way to the back of the house, intermingling with the faint sugar cinnamon smells still floating around in the kitchen.

Doña Fortunata told herself she would have to pay Andrés' mother a small visit tomorrow. Meanwhile, she watched Andrés pile his plate with the round, powdery *canela* cookies.

"Don't hurry, Andrés. Your work at home can wait. *Acomódate,* make yourself comfortable and eat slowly while I tell you a little story. *Este es un cuento nuevo.* It's about *brujería.* You will be the first to hear it . . .

A ver si te gusta. Let's see if you like it."

COCHITI CORN DANCE

Roberta Swann

It's a sight that makes me welcome. Why,
I can't say. I don't know the painted men
of Cochiti, wearing Hopi kilts with evergreen
arms, feathered, furred and foxtailed. Or
the women in black with tablitas on their heads.
They walk in pairs, from the kivas into the plaza.
Dancing one dance after another, they go on all day,
under blazing sun, changing sounds and rhythms,
like life itself—give and take, gifts and sacrifice.
A drummer keeps the heartbeat. Bells fall like rain.
Black and white striped clowns egg everyone on.
Spectators come and go. And I breathe in every dusty bit.
A grandmother offers us her shaded chairs.
Her grandson brushes by. His smaller sister
pulls his foxtail. She wants a snowcone too.
They sit under a cottonwood: "One star,
two star," she pokes, counting ice-crystals
in the cone he just licks. We walk toward
the car we can't locate. A man says
if we can't find it, it belongs to the pueblo.
"If we can't find it," I reply, "You're welcome."

Fire in the Hole

Roberta Swann

Beans take four hours to cook
at this altitude, but nature thrives
seven thousand feet up in these mountans.
So does my husband who keeps up a running
commentary on the wildlife, putting
words in their mouths. He tracks
droppings and points out pieces
of sunstruck resin. He's grouchy
because I can't read maps
without glasses, but in town
spot a tiny price tag on a $200
dress at a Donna Karan outlet.
He cries: It's a miracle.
She can see. Nothing bothers me
at this altitude, except construction
crews building a new house above us,
blasting jackhammers all day.
"Fire in the hole, fire in the hole,"
we hear before dynamite explodes.
My husband bolts from bed. I lie shaken.
Only later do I tell him the earth
finally moved.

LIES

Jana Giles

A lone plane drew a chalk mark beneath the moon. It was a gibbous moon and that meant close to the end and hunched over. The old man stepped out of his trailer listening to the twilight.

"No snow til next Wednesday!" he shouted in to his wife. She didn't answer and he didn't expect her to. The sky was clear and only one or two stars were out.

He was looking at the stone wall he was building, made of the limestone and sandstone rocks he had collected from the hills around his place. A rock and some cement. Another rock, some more cement. It was to be a low wall, because he didn't want to keep anything out, with small tapering pillars, two feet at the base, maybe one foot at the top, maybe four feet high. That was what he had in mind. Every day he added three rocks. That was all. He liked to work slow so that it would take a long time and look just like he wanted it to. After he did the wall he would think about building a house.

Someone was coming walking down the road. Ah, it's only Crazy Jimmy. The old man stood on the cinder block steps with his hands in his pockets waiting for him to get closer. When Jimmy was about twenty feet from his driveway he walked down to meet him.

"*Qué tal*, Jimmy. You still walking? It's getting cold. It's getting late."

"*Hola*," Jimmy said, lurching toward him. "*Un conejo. Un conejo.*"

Jimmy's eyes were permanently red in his dark face but the old man suspected he saw some juice welling up in the lids.

"What rabbit, Jimmy? I don't see no rabbit."

"*Conejo*," said Jimmy, pointing back along the road.

A dead rabbit? The old man peered down the highway. His eyes weren't too good. But his nose was good and he smelled something like meat just about to go bad.

"Oh no, Jimmy. Whatchu got in your jacket?"

"Abeet," Jimmy said, and now the old man knew he was crying because the moonlight reflected off a trail on his cheek. He smiled at the old man.

"You ought to brush your teeth sometime, Jimmy. You only got four left, better take care of them before they all fall out. *Saca el conejo*, Jimmy. *Sácalo del* jacket."

Jimmy usually did what the old man said when he understood him. He opened his brown corduroy jacket a little and exposed one arm cradling a dead rabbit that had been hit by a car. The rabbit's fur was torn around its head and it had bled from the mouth, nose and ears. It looked as if some crows had gotten to it. Jimmy's sweater was crusted with old blood and fur.

"No, no, Jimmy," the old man said gently. "The rabbit is dead. *El conejo está muerto.* You got to let him rest now, let him sleep. Don't bother that poor rabbit no more. Put him over here, under this tree."

But Jimmy would not let go of the rabbit and squeezed it up harder to his chest.

"Can I hold it?" the old man asked, stretching out his arms. Shit, Claudia is going to kill me. "Can I rock it to sleep?"

"Abeet," said Jimmy, grinning. He looked down at the rabbit in his arms as if he had just remembered it was there. He leaned over and dropped the rabbit in the old man's arms. The old man put it in the crook of his elbow, the way Claudia had told him to hold his grandchildren when they came out of the hospital. "Nice rabbit," he muttered. "*Duérmete ya.*"

"Pedro!" he heard his wife shout. "*¿Qué haces afuera?* It's cold out there!"

"I'm just talking to Jimmy, Okay? You want to wake up the neighbors?"

Just as he expected, Jimmy had forgotten about the rabbit and was pulling out one of his cigars. He offered Pedro one but the old man shook his head.

"I got to go now," he said, as Jimmy began wandering back down to the highway. Poor Jimmy, he thought, laughing, he's our fool and the rest of us, we're kings. He does his little dance down the highway for us. A bird, a tree, a stone, a rock, a bone. That's Jimmy's world. Someday he's going to get hit by a car in the night, his luck will run out. What the hell am I going to do with this rabbit? What is she going to do to me?

There were a couple of old cars scattered on his property, mostly old Fords so he could do a little repair work on his white pick-up. One of them was a sedan and had a trunk that was more or less together. He could throw the rabbit in there so the dogs couldn't get it and then he could burn it in the morning.

"What in the name of the unmentionable!" shouted Claudia when he went inside. "Get out of my kitchen! *¡Foh!* You stink like *una vaca podrida*! Take that thing off and put it somewhere."

"*¡Ay Dios!*" Pedro protested. "I was just going to take it off. Can't an old man think for himself? *¡Que me lléven los angelitos para poder estar en paz!*" He went out into the utility room and stripped off his padded plaid shirt. It smelled, but not that bad. Claudia was exaggerating everything, as usual. She'd smelled worse things. He shook it outside to get the big chunks off and washed his hands and arms in the sink.

"I wish the angels *would* drag you away, or the devils, or somebody. Then maybe I could get something done instead of waiting for you to get out of my way. *Tu café está* cold, you better drink it. And you haven't been to the *iglesia* in three weeks so you better quit talking about *El Señor* behind his back. He don't want you talking to him that way."

"Huh. At this time in my life I don't care what I do to get his attention. How do you know what he likes to hear? An old man has the right to say what he likes, he's just getting ready to die and go somewheres, that's all."

"You better be careful then, *viejo*. If you aren't he just might keep you alive longer than you expect. *Ten cuidado*."

She was right. The coffee was cold. He drank it like it was because he suddenly felt tired and did not want to get up. He knew she didn't want to get up either because she was old, and if he asked her to heat it up she would say that she was old and tired and would she have to ask *la Virgen* to tell him to let her rest? He knew her coffee was cold too because she always waited for him and it was his fault that he hadn't come inside and they both had to drink cold coffee. That was really why she had yelled at him about the shirt.

"What was this with Jimmy?" she asked. "Is that why you stink?"

"I don't know who's more tired, you or me, so I'll tell you tomorrow. Don't molest me anymore old woman."

They went to sleep and he dreamt that the rabbit jumped out of the trunk of a shiny new Cadillac and was fifteen feet tall. It didn't look like *Cristo* but he knew it was. He still knew it was *Cristo* when it began scratching at the house with its front claws even though he knew *Cristo* would never do such a thing. But then he got scared and wanted to scream because he was afraid he had tricked himself and this was not *Cristo* at all, but the devil. He realized how ridiculous everything was and laughed until hot tears rolled down his cheeks and he woke himself and Claudia up. She said something about the unmentionable and rolled over. Pedro stayed awake and lay on his back watching the early light change colors.

The next day he burned the rabbit first thing. He saw scratch marks on the rusty trunk of the car so he knew he'd been hearing the dogs in his dream. He went to the hardware store to pick up a U-joint for the kitchen sink because it was leaking. In the afternoon he added three stones to the wall and announced to Claudia that he was going to the Windmill to have a beer with the men. Alicia, their daughter, was sitting in the kitchen visiting. She was showing pictures of their three-year-old grandson to Claudia.

"*¡Mira qué* cute, hon!" Claudia crooned, holding up one of the photos for him to look at.

"Yeah, he's cute. I just saw him day before yesterday and he was cute then, too. He's going to get big soon and cause trouble and then he won't be so cute. I'm taking the truck."

"If you see Mario there," Alicia said, "tell him I will personally cut his balls off if he isn't home at eleven."

"*Bien*," Pedro said, "I will tell him."

So when he saw Mario standing at the counter, he delivered the message first thing to get it over with. "Alicia said she would remove your manhood if you aren't home at eleven."

"I told you that as soon as you get married it's a conspiracy," Mario said to Little Peter, who was sitting next to him. "Now even the old man is telling me he will cut my balls off!" He slapped Pedro on the back and bought him a Miller.

Evángelo was with them and greeted Pedro. He lived across the highway and was Jimmy's younger brother. He never did much except for road jobs when he could find them. In the fall he bought a permit to cut firewood in the mountains and sold it by the cord out of his truck in front of Gloria's Package Bar and Liquors, along with Gerónimo and Primitivo and the other men that had lived in the mountains all their lives, to the hippies when they first moved in and now the yuppies that drove back and forth to town everyday. Jimmy had his own lean-to built onto the house because Anita, Evángelo's wife, said he was dirty and wouldn't let him in her house. There were other brothers, too, but they had moved to the city and only came to visit on Christmas and Easter and Thanksgiving.

"Hey, I saw your crazy brother last night," Pedro said to Evángelo. "He had some dead rabbit."

"Damn that pig," said Evángelo, slamming down his beer. "No wonder he was stinking so much this morning. I had to take him his breakfast because Anita wouldn't do it. Did you tell him to throw it *al carájo*?"

"What do you think I did?" asked Pedro. "I smacked him around the head a little and told him to get the hell off my property with that thing." He left the bar to sit by the stone fireplace where a hot orange fire burned, filling the small room with the smell of cedar. Mario and Evángelo were laughing about Jimmy and him fighting over a dead rabbit.

He always told Claudia that he was going to have a drink with the men but in fact he usually sat alone at the fire after making the rounds. If Carmelo was there they sat together, two old men in their baseball caps blackened with grease. Carmelo was his oldest friend. In 1952 they had shot the biggest buck ever seen there, and they held the record until someone had broken it just a couple years ago. They had hunted him every other weekend of the season for three years. It was Carmelo's shot that killed him but he was generous enough to loan Pedro the head every other year. At the old man's house there was a big nail next to the wood stove saved just for the buck. When Claudia was out he would pat him and tell him his troubles. He stopped hunting when they got that one because he didn't like hunting that much anyway, and since he had got someone to talk to there didn't seem to be any point in continuing.

He sat alone at the fire. He was too old for the company of the younger men and he was sick of hearing Mario talk. Mario generally had nothing good to say, not even about his own family. Pedro could do nothing about it. He ordered another beer and thought about his wall. He figured it would take him through the summer to get the front done. Three rocks a day was enough for him, since some days the rocks were real heavy and took a lot of work to move. He did not want to grow so old that he would have to sit inside and watch his wall fall apart. He wanted to die building it.

Some bikers had come in and were crowding up the place.

"We come into this town where they weren't familiar with us," one of them was telling Mario and the others. "The guy in the store said, 'Spinal meningitis' when he saw us, and we couldn't figure out what spinal meningitis had to do with us. Then he said something else and we figured out that he'd said 'Smilin' mighty Jesus.'" Everyone roared and Evángelo fell off his stool. Pedro overheard Mario telling Little Peter through his laughing tears that he had kicked Pedro's oldest grandson out of the house for dropping out of high school just before he was about to graduate. That must have been why Alicia was at the house. The old man got up to leave.

"*Hasta luego*, Mario," he said, as he passed the bar. "Evángelo."

"*Nos vemos, viejo*. Tell Alicia I'll get home when I get there. Say hello to your old woman."

Pedro stepped out onto the stone porch. The snow had come early and ruined his predictions. It had just started falling while he was in the bar and he wished he had left the truck at the house so he could walk back.

"Lies," the old man muttered, staring at the orange glow of the fire from the window on the film of snow. "It's all a pack of lies."

Maybe I'll walk back anyway. An old man should do what he wants. He wondered if he should go back and tell them he was walking, but he knew they would laugh at him for bothering to tell them and then not let him go. He considered leaving a note in the truck but he had nothing to write with so he just left it like it was.

As he walked he wasn't cold at all, except that the cold beauty of the moon shifting behind the clouds shivered him a little. He couldn't see the stars, but the landscape was bright and soft and silent. There were blue shadows under the black and white junipers, and the hills looked like a deserted lunar landscape. There was no sound except for the crunch of his feet. Not many cars were on the road. When he stopped walking once or twice, he could barely hear the sound of the snow falling on itself, a tiny hiss not quite as soothing as the rain. This must be how Jimmy feels when he walks, he thought.

He was surprised, then, when an enormous jack-rabbit whose ears reached Pedro's shoulders hopped up and began loping alongside of him.

"Nice evening, isn't it," said the jack.

"Couldn't be better," replied the old man, who had no wish to be disagreeable even though his solitude was interrupted. "Not even that cold out. Who are you?"

"Who do you think?" said the jack, as if that were a really dumb question.

"I don't get it," said the old man, wondering if the rabbit was planning on being disagreeable by confusing him.

The rabbit raised its eyes to the heavens with a look of patient suffering.

"I am the one you talk to when you think you are just talking to yourself, and I am the one who dreams your dreams for you."

"But you were in my dreams last night. How can you dream my dreams and be in them at the same time?"

"In that case," said the jack, "how can I be dreaming your dreams and in your dreams and loping along beside you this very minute?" And it stopped a moment to lick the snow balls from one of its hind paws.

The old man stood there watching it, wondering if this idea of taking a walk was a bad one because he might be going crazy just like Jimmy. Without saying good-bye or anything the rabbit stopped licking itself and leapt away across the highway,

"I think you're gonna die now," it said to Pedro.

"Shit," Pedro said, as the truck swerved to avoid the rabbit, skidded on the slick asphalt, and struck him in the back, "I think you're right."

The jack watched as the truck stopped and two drunks stumbled out to peer at Pedro on the ground.

"¡Ay, qué he hecho!" cried Mario, horrified. "Holy fucking Christ! I thought it was Jimmy! I've killed the old man!"

The jack just shook its head sadly. "Some people never learn."

"Nope," Pedro agreed, "They never do."

Drought

Trebbe Johnson

In the summer of 1990, I received a small private grant to spend a month in northeastern Arizona doing research for a book about the Navajo-Hopi land dispute, an issue I had been studying and writing about for four years. My intention was to interweave about half a dozen points of view to tell the story of the 1974 law that ordered the partition of land both tribes held sacred and the relocation of everyone who subsequently found himself on the other tribe's land. Things did not work out the way I'd planned.

In the land "between sacred mountains," where the two distinctly different Hopi and Navajo cultures had lived side by side for more than five hundred years, the earth was thirsting. The worst fear of Hopi farmers had come to pass: the washes they depended upon to flow down to their cornfields from the forested upland of Black Mesa were dry. Arizonans would remember the summer of 1990 as the hottest and driest in living history. The Hopis blamed the drought not on the weather but on Peabody Coal Company, which pumped a billion and a half gallons of aquifer water a year in order to slurry coal from its strip mine on Hopi and Navajo lands through three hundred miles of pipeline to Nevada. Hopi religious leaders had warned that there would be consequences to pay for the desecration of this sacred female mountain. Now, the mountain was taking its revenge.

Dalton Taylor, a Hopi farmer and member of the Snake Society, who lives in the ancient village of Shungopavi, told me bluntly that no one was going to have time to talk to me. Humans had to perform the tasks the earth could not. Dalton himself rose before dawn each day to haul buckets of water out to the range where his cattle grazed. After filling the dry, caked catchment pond so the animals could drink, he would crawl under his truck to nap for a spell out of reach of the sun. Nearly every weekend, he attended ceremonies in his own and the other Hopi villages clustered on the edge of three high mesas; from dawn till nightfall, the dusty plazas rang with songs, drums, bells and rattles as the masked kachinas danced their prayers for rain.

The drought was personal as well as meteorological. Although the leaders of both tribal governments had banded together in an effort to urge Peabody to find an alternate means of transporting the coal, relations between Hopi and Navajo families had deteriorated since the passage of the law that was supposed to have settled the land dispute. Clifford Balenquah, a member of the Hopi tribal government, had hoped to build a home on the plateau beneath the mesas, land that had reverted to the Hopis, but that, he said bitterly, had proved impossible. Of the 10,000 people of both tribes affected by the relocation order, about 95 percent were Navajos, and many of them not only refused to vacate the land, but harassed any Hopi who ventured onto it.

Things were no better among the Navajos whose stories I had hoped to flesh out. Roberta Blackgoat, an elder from the community of Big Mountain, was recuperating from a cataract operation at her daughter's home in Flagstaff. When I first met Roberta in 1986 she had been robust and straight-backed, with a hearty sense of humor. Even though the law imposed such severe restrictions on the number of sheep she could have and even the kinds of repairs she could make on her hogan that several family members had had to leave home and move to town, she had refused to budge. "My roots go way down deep and can't be pulled out," she'd insisted. Now, sitting on the couch and watching television from behind dark glasses, she had the thin, dry-leaf voice of an old woman, her white hair had lost its sheen, and her face sagged.

I drove over to the winding ponderosa pine-lined Flagstaff street where Nora Talltree (not her real name) and her family lived. After years of resisting relocation, the Talltrees had finally concluded that they had no choice but to relocate, even though that meant Nora would be severing the tie to her ancestral land, a bond forged at birth when her father had buried her umbilical cord near the corral. The Talltrees had formed a support group for other relocatees, hoping that, by sharing their experiences, they could ease the pain and isolation that forced relocation invariably brought. But today Nora's skin was sallow and she moved slowly. She told me she had discovered a lump in her breast that tests showed to be malignant. She had had a lumpectomy, followed by two chemotherapy treatments, but the cure made her so sick she had decided to forego modern medical procedures altogether. Now she was seeing an acupuncturist and working with a Navajo medicine man. The medicine man believed the cancer had been caused by spiritual poison, which Nora had absorbed in her long fight against relocation.

After I left Nora's house, I drove to the Museum of Northern Arizona and went out back, where a self-guided trail meanders through high-desert country. It is comforting to walk a path marked by guideposts, but today, I had no sense of where I was headed. Interviewing Nora had made me sick. Over a period of four years I had become familiar with her struggle to fight the law; her worry about her mother, who remained on the land, and her children, who were forgetting their native language; her depression when relatives and neighbors relocated to town and, separated from their land, families, ceremonies, plants and animals, simply lost the will to live. I had glimpsed her shame after she had done the one thing she vowed she'd never do: taken the government's money for a new house. Today, I had looked down at the tape recorder efficiently soaking up her words and felt I could no longer summon up Nora's or anyone's else's pain for my edification. Still, I had this grant. I had a book to write. I did not know what I was going to do.

I had started writing about the Navajo-Hopi land dispute because I was appalled that people who knew so well how to live on the land were being forced to leave it. I hoped that by calling attention to what was happening, I might help prevent a cultural crisis with ecological implications, and, at the same time, give people from my own acquisitive, image-conscious white society a glimpse of two peoples who placed supreme value on their relationship with the earth. My trips to Hopi and Navajo country were journeys into people's hearts.

When I would show up at their door, a white stranger with pads, pen and a tape recorder, they were wary. At first they would answer my questions in terse, cautious sentences, not wishing to be rude, yet determined to give nothing of themselves away. Then something extraordinary would happen: they began to unfold like a parched plant to the refreshing truth of their own experience. They ceased talking to me and talked simply because there was so much that needed to be told. Sometimes they would catch themselves and ask me not to print something they'd said, but then they would go on as before, the need to speak having grown bigger than the need for discretion.

My own role in this process was not entirely guileless. Although I did not try to incite people to despair, nostalgia, outrage, and fear, I did nothing to stanch such emotions when they arose. I sat quietly, trying to be invisible, the impulse to comfort held in check by my fear that the eloquent passion I was listening to would cease if I called attention to it or to myself, who really had no right to witness it. How these men and women felt when, at last, I drove away and they were left with their emotions spilled all over the place is one of the questions I never asked.

Both I, the interviewer, and those I interviewed behaved as if journalism was the only thing happening between us. I was writing a story, they had information to impart, and for this exchange we had consented to enter into a temporary business partnership. But underneath, each of us longed for something more. Almost everyone I spoke with complained that the true story of the land dispute had never been properly told. What they meant, of course, was that no one had told *their* truth, and what they hoped was that I would set down accurately not just their words, but their very souls. If that could happen, they believed, the outside world would understand the situation at last and be moved to insist that it be changed. To some that change was repeal of the law, to others it was the eviction of the Navajos, or the banning of industry from

Indian land, or the replacement of the white-style tribal councils with traditional leadership—there were countless visions of the ideal future. As for me, I, too, had an idea of how things ought to be different, and it wasn't strictly limited to the land dispute.

"Our life is our religion and our religion is the land," a 21-year-old Navajo man told me once after we had spent the day at Big Mountain and were eating cheeseburgers in a Flagstaff mall. I wished I could say the same. Like a growing number of people, I believed that the only way we could solve our dire environmental problems was to treat the earth as reverently as if it were the living, sacred entity indigenous people had always said it was. Or, as the Catholic theologian Thomas Berry had written in *The Dream of the Earth,* "The universe itself, but especially the Planet Earth, needs to be experienced as the primary mode of divine presence." I wanted to learn how to listen to the infinite voices of the earth, how to respect the earth not just by treading softly upon it, but also by paying homage to it in some way, how to go through the day as if all my tasks were holy.

Over hundreds of years, the Hopi and Navajo people had cultivated ways of living on the land that served them well in both mystical and practical ways. Like most traditional Navajos, Roberta Blackgoat regarded her sheep as a gift from the Holy People. To protect them, she would smoke medicinal plants in a fire and herd the animals through it while she sang prayers. She knew how to care for the sheep when they were sick, how to butcher them for food (after offering some of the blood back to the earth), and how to weave the wool into beautiful rugs whose patterns reflected the forms of land and sky. What the nomadic, herding life was to the Navajos agriculture was to the Hopis, descendants of the ancient Anasazi culture. From the time Dalton Taylor had received initiation into the first Hopi religious society as an adolescent boy, he had been learning a complex cosmology in which the universal energies of germination and growth were mirrored in the Hopi cornfields. Throughout the year, he was actively involved in a series of elaborate ceremonies whose purpose was to pray for the well-being of all creatures and, on a microcosmic scale, for rain to nourish the corn that flourished so well in this land of little rain that agriculturalists from all over the world came to study it.

Vine Deloria, a Standing Rock Sioux author and University of Colorado professor, whose book, *God is Red,* explores the fundamental differences between the spiritual worldview of Native people and Judeo-Christians, had told me impatiently once when I interviewed him for a magazine article, "You white people need to find your own traditions. They're out there. You don't need ours." But my grandparents, farmers and gardeners all, had no prayers for the earth, at least none that they ever taught me. And anyway, it is this land I belong to, this United-States-of-American land, not Sweden or Norway, whence my ancestors hailed. Much as I would have loved to learn from them who knew the earth was alive, they have been dead a long time and they have left no record of how they worshipped. The Navajo and Hopi people had that direct teaching, and, what is more, they practiced it still.

I was not alone in being drawn to their worldview. In the mid-80s, scores of people came to Navajo-Hopi country to volunteer their services on behalf of the Indian people whom they believed were being victimized by the federal government, energy interests, and their own progressive tribal council leaders. But it was more than a need to right a political injustice that impelled people to leave college, jobs, and families and come out west to work long hours without pay. Saddened by the toxic pall over their cities, the dubious quality of their drinking water, and reports of disappearing forests and vanishing species, and feeling powerless to halt the course of destruction, they, too, thirsted for a bond with the natural world that would be more meaningful than simply sorting their recyclable garbage each week.

Therefore, while some sympathizers concentrated on lobbying, fund raising, and doing clerical work in the activist Big Mountain Legal Office in Flagstaff, others had determined that their services must consist of nothing less than going up to the land to live with Navajo elders and help them with chores, while absorbing their way of life. The Navajos accepted with grace as much as gratitude, joking privately about volunteers who panicked when a sheep started giving birth or who fled for home with a heavy stomach after a steady Navajo diet of mutton, fry bread and strong coffee laced with sugar. Ivan Sidney, the Hopi tribal council chairman from 1982 to 1990, was convinced that non-Indian volunteers were inciting the Navajos to disobey the law by staying on the land. Noting that some of them sported Indian-style windbands and beaded jewelry, and adopted names like Swaneagle and Little Bear, he condemned them as "Wanna-be's." They insisted, however, that they did not "wanna be" Indian. "These old women are completely different from the grandmothers in our white society," said a young woman, who had spent several weeks with one of the elders of Big Mountain. "They stand against the BIA (Bureau of Indian Affairs) police, against relocation, against the policies of the energy companies. These women are living there with the earth. They are bonded with the animals, the plants, the mountains. Their lives have become real hard. I came to help them and to get an education from them."

By the summer of 1990, the energy of the issue had sputtered like a broken-down old pickup. The law was still in effect, there were still Navajos living on the land that had been partitioned to the Hopis, and relocation was still destroying individual lives and ancient traditions. The volunteers had drifted on to other causes. Reporters and photographers who had covered the issue amidst rumors that the National Guard might be summoned to haul elderly sheepherders off the land had lost interest once the colorful footage had faded into a black-and-white still of exhausted people waiting for change. Maybe the oppressive heat made things worse, but it seemed to me that both peoples just wanted to be left alone to carry on their lives. The imperatives of getting water to the cattle and regaining personal health had forced them to shift their attention away from the endless problem of the land dispute and concentrate instead on raw physical survival. This may even have been a relief.

Dalton Taylor was right: most people were unable or unwilling to talk to me about the land dispute, an issue that had become as oppressive, stagnant and impervious to human will as the relentless hot weather. I had to wonder if my own reluctance to dredge up their pain might not also be responsible in some karmic way for the swath of missed appointments and excuses I kept encountering.

And so, for the first time since I'd been traveling in Hopi-Navajo country, I had free time. One thing I did was explore the land. No matter where you stand on the land between sacred mountains, you comprehend, on a visceral rather than an intellectual level, how the myths about the place arose and why the indigenous people consider it sacred. On previous trips I had rarely ventured beyond the driver's seat of my rental car, as I covered the miles from one hogan, one Hopi village, to another, packing in as many interviews as I could. Now I hiked in the San Francisco Peaks and Oak Creek Canyon, tracked wild elk across the undulating grassland of Garland Prairie, visited Anasazi sites, and joined a local botanist on a trek to identify medicinal plants. One day Nora Talltree took me to Blue Canyon, where she had grown up. She and her daughter Amy and I stood in one spot, midway between the flat, treeless land above the earth and the canyon floor below, and Nora told stories. She told about the mythological holy being, Changing Woman, walking the length of the canyon to collect offerings people had left for her; about Navajo families who made their homes at the foot of those tall red cliffs and whose ways were so traditional that they still got around by horse and wagon; about the blue-green clay her mother had scooped from the earth and molded into people and animals for the children to play with; about the time some herders had seen a spaceship land on a flat grassy area that was so marked by the phenomenon that nothing had grown there since; about the days she and her sisters had spent here herding sheep and exploring the recesses, niches and furbelows in the rock; and about an ancient shrine where they had found brilliant parrot feathers and the charred remains of an offering of corn. I realized sadly that non-native Americans could never reach such a profound multi-dimensional experience of a place. Even those who have lived on a farm for many generations and who have acquired both knowledge of and love for the land, have no creation myths or stories of epic events to suffuse local land forms with numinous energy. Moreover, although I was convinced that many non-Indians had experienced mysterious and heartfelt interactions with animals, plants, soil and rivers, they rarely spoke of them, perhaps thinking them either figments of their imagination or a sign of mental instability.

Besides exploring the land, I did what I could to be of use. I brought groceries to Roberta Blackgoat at her daughter's house and stayed to watch a video of "The Bear" with Roberta and her two little great-granddaughters; drove a Hopi elder around the BIA's official labyrinth so he could get information about the use of Hopi water by outside interests; and spent weekends attending ceremonies on the Hopi mesas. I was surprised how hard it was at first to tuck in my journalistic antennae, always buzzing to pick up clues, and to quit trying to be invisible.

One night, a friend of mine, a former easterner who had moved to Flagstaff after a single visit to the Grand Canyon, listened while I tried to unravel the problem of whether whites desperate for an earth-based spirituality were violating native people by trying to imbibe theirs. "Our ancestors knew the earth was sacred, too," she said, and got up to search her bookcase. That night in my little cabin, I started reading *The Death of Nature: Women, Ecology and the Scientific Revolution* by Carolyn Merchant. Merchant traces European attitudes toward the natural world from the Middle Ages and Renaissance, when the whole earth was conceived as a living female body, fecund and mysterious, to the late 17th century, when the invention of earth-moving forges, windmills, and pumps encouraged the view that nature was a mechanism that could not only be understood but controlled. I was amazed to learn that it had not been millennia, as I had assumed, but only a few hundred years, since a divine presence had been as immanent in the forests and fields of Europe as it was today in the land between sacred mountains. For example, the popular Renaissance image of the earth's anatomy, in which ore flowed through her subterranean veins, gold germinated in her womb, and gases built up pressure in her bowels until they burst as earthquakes, made me think of Roberta Blackgoat's designation of Black Mesa, where the coal was being mined, as the liver of Mother Earth. Paracelsus, the 16th century Swiss physician and alchemist, taught that every facet of the cosmos was imbued with astral spirit, a substance that came originally from the stars and provided humans with a direct and conscious link to the divine plan. This sense of the ongoing viability of the germ of creation was similar to the Hopi belief that every ceremony literally re-enacted and renewed the universal creative process.

And the Hopi and Navajo view that all aspects of nature are brothers and sisters whose life profoundly affects each other earthly being, had a counterpart in the theory of Vitalism put forth by Anne Conway, a 17th century Englishwoman, who tried to combat the emerging mechanistic worldview by arguing that each creature had a "central or governing spirit" and that all beings "mutually subsist one by another, so that one cannot live without another."

It is true, unfortunately, that by the time Bernardino Telesio of Italy was writing that God was omnipresent in nature and that all matter was alive, his late countryman, Christopher Columbus, had enslaved the Arawak peoples of the Caribbean and forced them to desecrate their sacred mountains to supply him with gold. Moreover, even the pantheistic theories of the Europeans were filtered through the fundamental tenets of Judeo-Christian monotheism, so they reflected the assumption of human superiority set forth in Genesis, when God cast Eve and Adam out of Eden, exhorting them to have dominion over "the fish of the sea, over the birds of the air, and every living thing that moves on the earth". For instance, in Conway's metaphysics, there was a hierarchical chain of being in the universe, in which each entity, from dust to humans, could attain increasingly high levels of perfection. This glorification of progress runs counter to the native view that each being already perfectly fulfills its role in the cosmic web of life. Still, I was delighted to know that, not so long ago, my ancestors had regarded trees and rivers as entities imbued with spirit. It put me in closer relation to *their* ancestors, tribal people who had danced around sacred fires to propitiate the deities of thunder and lightning, who had followed strict codes of behavior when the imminence of the harvest or the hunt meant life or death for the community, who had requested guidance from birds and animals—and received it.

Not long after I began to hear the echo of my ancestors' footsteps on the earth, a Hopi friend who knew of my fondness for sleeping outside, gave me directions to a canyon north of Oraibi, on land where his family had grazed their cattle since his grandmother's day. The canyon was a long narrow rip of earth that zigzagged farther to the west than I felt inclined to follow (although I wondered if it might eventually link up with Nora's Blue Canyon) and was about as wide as a New York City block. The sand at the bottom was soft and white and held the prints of coyotes and snakes. In places the rock walls, colored like bread, blood, and honey, had tumbled down on top of one another. Juniper and pinyon trees had improbably taken root among them, and thrust out over the space below like the necks of curious mountain goats. Nothing of the world beyond the rim was visible except turquoise sky. As the turquoise faded to pale blue, then gray, swallows darted through the channel of sky on last important errands. Then a great emptying took place—of light, warmth, flight, color, sound—and finally the stars began to emerge. Slowly, the moon, a couple of days past full, made its way through the boughs of a juniper tree, cleared it, and shone down. I did a dance of gratitude to the place for allowing me to see its beauty, and then I wriggled into my sleeping bag on the sand.

When I woke the moon had arced high above the canyon. Its light silvered the sand and the tips of yucca blades on the rim, and showed darkness pooled in the hollows of the rocks. Inches above my head, a cricket sang. Cradled in the canyon, I felt the abounding presence of many forces of nature, including those I could not see, like the cricket, or even hear, like the animals stepping softly, searching for food, and the physical forces that whirled in the rocks, holding them up or urging them to let go and plunge. Overhead the stars slowly revolved, predictable and incomprehensible. And at that moment I knew nothing so well as I knew how the first humans who woke to consciousness and stood shivering before the mystery of life had recognized the earth as their original and most divine mother.

Before dawn, when night was still thick in the west, and the sky a starless charcoal smudge in the east, I crawled up out of the canyon on all fours and sat on a rock to await the sun. It was a long wait, the modulations of light so subtle as to be almost unnoticeable. At one moment I was seized with panic that this might be the one dread day when the sun would not appear. When the first rays pierced the brightening haze over the horizon I was exhilarated. Now the sun was no enforcer of drought but the giver of radiant life after the night that was gestation in the womb of the earth.

From the Hopi and Navajo people I learned a great deal about how spiritual theories and practical tasks are indivisible when you enact them in a sacred place, permeated with abundant, vital energy. I also saw how even that potent energy, which has accrued over hundreds of generations of conscious interaction between people and nature, can be extinguished when federal laws restrict such simple but ancient practices as building a hogan or when industries use abundant stores of water while native cornfields wither. Over four years, I was honored to attend ceremonies vastly older than any Christian or Jewish rite ever celebrated on this continent, to visit sacred places and hear stories of their origin, to eat meals by lamplight, and sleep on a pile of sheepskins, and to hear in countless eloquent ways how people love and take care of the land that has taken care of them.

But the details of Navajo and Hopi life were not what influenced my own behavior toward the earth. I do not say Hopi and Navajo prayers or enact Hopi and Navajo ceremonies, and I have not transplanted Hopi and Navajo cosmology to northeastern Pennsylvania, where I live with my husband. Rather, I gained from the people I met the faith that nature is alive, and that it communicates to anyone who acts respectfully toward it and is willing to listen to it. I understand now that, although we non-Indians lack a mythology of our place on this continent, we still have access to the land's unique energy, including most especially the land where we live. On my own land, for example, I can make it a point to learn the age of the rocks, the quality of the soil and the special properties of the plants, so that rocks and plants and soil become as co-inhabitants of the place, with needs and habits and propensities. I can imagine as I walk in the woods behind my house the footsteps of the animals and the indigenous people who preceded me. And I can note the sites where significant events occur on the land—not just natural events, but also those that lace together the human spirit and the spirit of the place: from the dead poplar branch in the pond where a blue heron perched to scan the water for frogs, to the patch in the shade of the house where the last of the snow melts in spring, to a place in the meadow where a friend played her cello one gray autumn Saturday. All this knowledge and imagination—all this attention—becomes the point on which the land's sacredness pivots, for these places become more fully enriched with meaning every time I recollect the events that happened there and share them with others.

DESERT VARNISH   *Bret Streeter*

Barnyard

Peter Wild

In the morning the rancher gets up
                    so light-headed
        he must have been up late reading Emerson.
    He steps not flesh but water aglow
                            into his boots
        which take him as usual
                    where he wants to go.
Out there dazed for a moment
                    because business will be good
    he considers the evidence, the air
    a cool liquid on his skin and all around
                the sky the pale blue of albumen,
meaning that the same stars
                    that swirled over Concord
        have just gone down,
                that huge family of sisters
    who though flat-chested once again
            have discovered they're madly in love,
while all the barnyard animals
            come up, flocking around him
    chirping and crooning,
                their eye shadow the work of amateurs
        slipping off, and the hearts
                    they cut out and pinned on
            crooked over where their real hearts belong,
    like children or pets, creatures
                you could love, even after death
        remembering their antics,
    having just escaped from the caves of Lascaux
                                as he did,
        and all together wanting to know how to be men.

MILLIONAIRES

Peter Wild

Today's clouds we stop to point at
                  must be God's thoughts
          floating over the earth,
                      so large, so brilliant
    we have no idea what they are.
  No doubt, up there
           He can see us far below,
      stick figures on our bicycles
                dipping across His countryside,
      or clinging to the rock
                never more in love.
It can drive you a little crazy
            watching them too much,
     what we saw a photographer
   taking a picture of, to make post cards
people would send around the world
                    to others who'd say
        this place can't be that good
      though it is, and he becomes a millionaire,
    as you do after dinner pausing
                  hand plunged behind your left ear
            for just one second in the kitchen
           thinking about this.

Discovering a Christian Hymnal: Winter 1980

Albino Carrillo

In the suburbs
I read a cruel pamphlet.
Its gray cover
announced safety in basements.

I read it with a girl one afternoon.
She believing in Christ stopped—
our explorations stopped,
revealing millions asleep
under the suicide sky. That night

the air was unhealthy,
cars and chimneys choking out
the invisible monoxide, citizens
singing Yuletide at the grocery store.

I imagined miles up
swarms of winter sparrows
returning to Mexico.

In the desert beyond Arroyo del Oso
boys rode up to bonfires on dirt bikes.
They warmed their hands
and drank from a shared
bottle of whiskey stolen that morning.

In the hills
developers with names like
falling branches were building
new homes daily. Whole families
grew up in subdivisions
unafraid of the desert, not knowing
the shell sky is an upturned
Mexican tin mirror frame.

Anyone leaving his house
would not be lonely. Strangers
quickly began to understand:
the new shadows of swallows
arrived while the neighbors turned
their soft voices
to each other like radio announcers.
They didn't know the dark
animal of loneliness speaking through them,
the constellations tumbling into morning.

The Placenta

Laurie Kutchins

After he has fallen asleep, after the last nursing
at the end of the undulant dusk when Venus has grown into a solitary
glitter in the western sky and his lips still tug at my nipple,
dreaming it into the smooth cave of his mouth as I carry him
sprawled out and limp from so much milk, as I move and stop
on each step to keep the sleep intact, toward the loft
where the shadows of dusk still shine on the cabin logs;
after I bend to lay him down, careful not to break the deep
and rhythmical breath, careful to transfer the feel of my arms
into the flannel I pack around him, cloth that smells of my milk
and high summer and him;
after I watch the eyelids quiver, the lips smack,
the small limbs flinch and stretch as if to awaken but this is
his body settling into the arms of night; then I am free
to go back down the steps and step outside,
and in the first full gasp of nightfall I find I am still thinking
about the placenta,
how strong and sinewy it was, how fast the doctor pulled it out
with rubber gloves and forceps made to fit a baby's head before it was
ready to leave, how he treated it like something worthless
and foul, medical rubbish to be quickly analyzed and disposed of,
when, in fact, I know it should have been paused over, admired, touched
and blessed; I look at the stars forming their nests overhead
and wonder, are you up there somewhere, sure of us
like an angel, like another child I made and lost?

Afternoon Along the Firehole River

Laurie Kutchins

Lying face up in the grass
that grows thick along the Firehole River, I am surrounded
by the amber births
of dragonflies.

Ravenous, like a string of sixteenth notes, they speed
up and down, feeding on things I cannot see
on the surface of the
warm current.

Thinking my nose is a sure stone, one pauses momentarily there—
I see close-up wings as sheer as a dress
I would wear made of 1920's
silk crepe.

They leave no sound in the eardrum of the afternoon.

I feel the present breeze on my forearms, then the deep snows,
the hooves and tongues of animals
who in the dead
of winter

find the river, its heat, its perfect islands of grass, and stand
with forelegs pressed against the rush
and piss
and drop their necks to the green mirage

of summer. I feel the tongues of the first trappers
who trapped themselves in this water
and in one breath blessed
and cursed it.

This is death licking me all over
until I rise wobbly and
unsure of the summer air, and enter
the river,
half fire from inside the earth, half snow melt.

My head drops into the braid of it, my body flows out
beyond me, my old shape in the grass
gleaming and strewn and
weightless
among the various husks.

COSAS, INC.

José Esquinas

It was ten o'clock on an April morning, the Taos sun already blinding on the pale stucco of my little bookstore. I shielded my eyes against the glare, managed to get the key in the padlock, but the heavy chain slipped through my shaky hands and cascaded with nerve-jangling clangor through the wrought-iron bars of the gate. Head pounding, I hurried to the storeroom and grabbed a couple of boxes and scurried back to the street to empty my books from one of the building's two adjacent display windows. This window belonged to the building's other retail space; the landlord allowed me to use it, as well as my own window, as long as I was the only tenant.

But now new tenants, new neighbors, were due to move in this morning, and I wanted to have the window ready for them when they came. It had been a long and lonely winter for me, and I wanted to be hospitable and avoid giving them the impression that they were pushing me out.

I hauled the boxed books (travel guides to New Mexico and the Southwest, Tony Hillerman mysteries, the obligatory D.H. Lawrence novels), down to my store, flung myself into my old swivel chair, poured myself a nip of the hair of the dog, and waited. A few minutes later, they pulled up outside in a white panel van. There were three of them: a tall, sandy-blond man, a black-eyed woman in jeans and a plain white blouse, and a mahogany-dark, very young man dressed in busily brilliant Guatemalan Indian costume. I took a deep breath and went down the hall to introduce myself.

The tall man could have been anywhere from his late twenties to his early forties. He held himself crookedly, as if his body had been broken and ill-fitted back together. His complexion was pitted and waxen, his lip sculpted in a fixed sneer above his eyetooth. His eyes shifted like two green buttons about to leave their red-stitched buttonholes. He introduced himself as Ernesto Dreyfus. His wife, Susana.

"Jaguar jew," she murmured. I had to think a few moments to realize this meant "how are you?" The expression on her swarthy, round face was as reticent as her husband's.

The Indian carried an enormous burden of colorful clothing on his back, which he gingerly deposited on the floor by bending over backwards and releasing the tumpline from his forehead. Seeing that the Dreyfuses were not going to introduce me to him, I stuck out my hand. He gave me a dead-fish shake, murmured his name—Archimedes—and dropped his timid gaze to his feet; they looked shrivelled and cold in his enormous tire-soled sandals. Susana said something to him in abrupt Spanish and he hurried back out to the van.

"Beautiful stuff," I said, rubbing the cochineal-red fabric between my fingers.

Susana gave me a tenuous smile, but Ernesto was scanning the room anxiously and didn't acknowledge my comment.

"Hey, how about a toast," I said. "Come on over to my place, we'll toast to your arrival." I raised an invisible shot glass to my lips. "Tostada? Tequila?"

"Ah," said Ernesto, his look of enlightenment turning quickly to one of pain. "Ah. Thank you very much. Yes. Later? Yes?"

"Little too early, huh," I agreed with mock guilt.

"Too early, yes, early!" said Ernesto. "Thank you."

They turned to each other and began setting up shop. The marimba over here, no, over there; all the blouses together and the skirts next to them; these trouble dolls will go on the counter. Their shingle went up: *Cosas*, carved in Gothic lettering. *Cosas*—Things. Not very catchy, I might have told them, had they asked my opinion, which they didn't. Indeed, they asked nothing of me at all, or about me, or about my shop, or the building, the landlord, Taos, nothing. They ignored me.

"So how'd you guys get into this business?" I finally asked.

They glanced at each other and did not answer.

"So who makes all this?" I said, my voice a little louder. "Most of it's hand made, isn't it?" I was growing disproportionately angry. What was the matter, did they think I was being intrusive? Were they unable to stop and chat for a moment, for the sake of what most people call neighborliness?

"*Quiché*," Ernesto replied in a low voice, pulling a stack of frightful masks from a box. "Guatemala. Indian, Indian," he added impatiently.

I could feel a prickling run across the lining of my brain; my face got hot. I ambled down to my end of the hall, glancing back just in time to catch Ernesto's hard jade gaze following me. The man's eyes shifted then and he raised a cautious arm, more a gesture of defense or rebuff, it seemed to me, than a wave.

Thirteen days would pass before Ernesto bothered to pay a visit to my store: I counted them with a kind of sour satisfaction, growing every day more irritated by the briskness of their business, by the falseness of the laughter they used with their customers, by the overly open vowels of their mercantile bonhomie. In the meantime, I put aside my poetry—I had come to Taos to write, the bookstore merely a means to keep the wolf from the door—and began to read what few titles I had on Guatemala. Apparently the place was populated mostly by impoverished Indians and ruled by people of European or mixed blood—*Ladinos*, the latter were called. I read one story about an Indian servant whose sole job was to get into the bed of his *Ladino* master and warm it up for half an hour before the master retired, and another about *Ladino* merchants who required young Indian slaves as loan collateral. Guatemala, it seemed, was a rather feudal place.

I poked my head out of my store between readings to observe the two *Ladinos* and their Indian. Archimedes' main job, in those first days, was to keep bringing load after load of goods on his back from the van— a name like that, I thought wryly, and they don't even allow him the leverage of a dolly. When once I beheld, astonished, Ernesto and Susana hunkered humbly beneath similar burdens, I decided it must be something of a show: they were trying to demonstrate solidarity with their Indian helper, for the gratified consumption of any egalitarian gringos who might be observing. But who did they think they were fooling? Not me!

The day Ernesto finally came in, I had been sitting at my desk, sipping Cuervo and trying to read a new title I had ordered: *I, Rigoberta*, the autobiography of the Nobel Peace Prize-winning Quiché Indian leader, Rigoberta Menchú. But my concentration was shot by my neighbors' trying to fob a plunky marimba off onto a loud and jolly Texan, and I slammed the book shut on the desk and watched the sunlit motes swirl madly, flashing like the synapses in my enraged mind. At last the Texan boomed an hasta la vista, and a few minutes later Ernesto entered my store in his wary, lupine way, big nose twitching: sniffing around.

"Well, well! Ernesto! So how's tricks?"

He gave a crooked smile."Tricks?"

I got up, upsetting my little dish of tequila salt, my head thickly buzzing. "Yeah, how's business? Isn't that what you're all about?"

He peered at me with curiosity, then shrugged bonily and made a smoothing gesture with his hands. "You have to make money."

"Why, sure you do. The business of America is business! So why don't you do it right? Why don't you throw a grand opening? Kind of let folks in the community know you're here."

"Is not necessary, I think," he said airily.

He was so sure of himself, and so dismissive of me!

"Well, Ernesto, you know what *I* think? I think you don't want to be a part of the community. I think yours is just another fly-by-night tourist operation into making a quick buck. That's what I think."

He was looking at me now with a patronizing, raised-eyebrow skepticism which infuriated me even more. I snatched the Menchú book and thrust it under his nose. "You're so wrapped up working for the Yankee dollar you probably don't even know what's going on in your own country. You should read this."

Ernesto didn't take the book; he just kept looking at me, the sneer trembling above his left canine. "You have read? Then you know much." And with that he walked out.

The Guatemalans, I noticed, fooled with their window display a lot, that window I had so conscientiously cleaned out for them that first day. They hung their jipijapa hats here, now there, they draped their sashes this way and that over the little backstrap loom, they fiddled with the flutes. One bright morning as I arrived to open my store, I found Ernesto's lanky frame hunched in the window; he was trying to get a pair of gourd rattles to stand up against each other.

I knocked sharply on the glass in taunting greeting, and he whirled to face me, kicking over the loom. He crouched there for a moment in a frozen lunge, like a creature—*Homo economicus* var. *retailensis?*—stuck in a museum diorama. I had to laugh. Later that day, as I kept picturing his startled face in the window, I got an idea.

I ordered nearly every title I could find on Guatemala and its strife. Then I emptied my window of its southwestern titles and filled it with these new ones: Payeras' *Days of the Jungle*, which described in hair-raising detail the beginning of the rural guerrilla movement in Guatemala; *Bitter Fruit*, an account of the United Fruit Company's and the CIA's depredations there; Amnesty International and Americas Watch reports documenting political disappearances and torture; more copies of the Menchú book. For good measure, I threw in Guillén's *Philosophy of the Urban Guerrilla*, the *Diary of Che Guevara*, and Castro's *Collected Speeches*. For the backdrop, I hung posters of Che and Zapata, and, in the center, a giant one hailing Guatemala's Guerrilla Army of the Poor: fist with raised rifle, fiery red background, a total call to arms. Standing back after my labors were done, I was pleased to hear a passing tourist voice drawl, "Why, it's an ad for the goddamn revolution!"

Ernesto's anticipated second visit was not long in coming. He wandered in at about the time he normally went to the bank to make his daily deposit—he already had his blue bank bag with him, in fact, tucked tenderly into his waistband. He nodded gravely at me, and began to peruse some of my new radical titles, prominently displayed on a table at the front of the store.

"You thought it was just window dressing, so to speak, didn't you?" I said with what I hoped was a galling joviality. "Well, you're wrong, *señor*. This is serious." I indicated, with a sweeping gesture, an entire bookcase of political titles.

Ernesto nodded again and continued to examine the new books, glancing up at me every now and then with a half-questioning expression. Something on the tip of his tongue; I predicted that he was just about to wheedle. Request, as politely as possible, that I tone things down. Say he agreed with a lot of this stuff, he really did, deep down, but that one had to be practical in this life. That this could not possibly be good for either of our businesses. That I knew as well as he how conservative were the times and the country we lived in, that the public would begin to think of our building as a Red center, to be avoided accordingly. And as I continued to smile smugly at him, the man was going to lose it. He was going to reveal his true colors, he was going to call it all garbage, subversion, he was going to froth at the mouth the way the ruling class of his country always frothed at the Communist Menace, and he was going to march his unglued self out in a tremendous huff.

But he didn't. All he did was flip through a couple more books, and then glanced with feigned surprise at his watch.

"Ah!" he said, tapping its face. "Bank!"

I was left smirking in the breeze of his departure. Bastard!

After a couple of weeks of seriously declining sales, I almost declared my point made and returned my bookstore to its former condition. But I stuck to it a little while longer, and that is when I noticed something fantastic beginning to happen: a completely new clientele was showing up regularly at my place. I hadn't known it before, but there existed in the area a fellowship of people with a deep and abiding interest in Latin American politics. They included committed artists and musicians from Taos and Santa Fe and the San Luis Valley in Colorado, graying La Raza militants from Las Vegas, Latin American Studies students from Albuquerque, and they were appearing at my bookstore, not just to browse and buy, but to meet each other and post fliers and converse with me about the state of the world. I felt a community in the making, and for the first time since arriving in Taos, I began to feel a real sense of usefulness and belonging. And with this new sense of things I began to let up on the booze. Alcohol, as one of my visitors had occasion to mention, was counter-revolutionary.

My hostility to the Dreyfuses, whom I now referred to as "those petty bourgeois elements down the hall," remained unabated, however, and I was delighted to learn that they were searching for another location for their shop (which was not going to be easy to find in Taos in the middle of summer). I envisioned, if I could somehow scrape the money together, taking over their space and coverting it into some kind of people's coffeehouse. It was also, I believed, my political and moral obligation to enlighten Archimedes about his situation, and about Guatemalan politics in general (I had read that the Indians were notoriously uninterested in politics at a national level, and considered them a *Ladino* thing); perhaps I could even succeed in luring him away from the Dreyfuses and into my new "community." So one day, during the afternoon doldrums when the Dreyfuses were out looking at real estate, I went over to visit Archimedes. I found him sitting on a stack of fabric, staring off into space, his spidery fingers rapidly weaving a jipijapa hat. He smiled broadly at me, his fingers not missing a move. Though my Spanish is not good, and he was not much of a talker, he spoke slowly and clearly, if cautiously, and I did manage to learn a few things about him. For one, he apparently hadn't known the Dreyfuses for long; he had hitched up with them in Los Angeles only a few days before they decided to come out to Taos. For my purposes, this was good, as it suggested that he didn't owe them any particular loyalty. He also, as I had suspected, didn't seem to know much about the political situation in Guatemala, or at least he wasn't letting on that he did. I invited him to come down to my bookstore, and as there were no customers at *Cosas* at the moment, he consented.

I showed him the Menchú book, and he studied her picture on the cover. I had read that a Guatemalan Indian can tell the very village where another is from from the patterns and colors of the other's clothing, and I contemplated him indulgently as he tried to so place her.

Then I tried to tell him the Menchú story, about how her father had been burned alive by government soldiers, and how her brother and mother had been "disappeared" and tortured, just because they asked for their rights and because they were thought to associate with people the government believed to be communists. The government of Guatemala was extremely harsh with Indians suspected of association with the "subversives," I warned him; and then I went on vividly to describe, miming where my Spanish failed me, the many tortures reserved for its enemies, from the crude (I feigned blows to his solar plexus) to the sophisticated (I unplugged a lamp and held the cord to my gums and crotch to show where the electric shocks were applied). There was the *ahogadito*, the "little drowning," in which water, optionally spiked with chile or ammonia, is forced up the prisoner's nose; then there was the *caballito*, in which the prisoner is forced to straddle a narrow pole; I even felt a twinge in my sinuses and little pang in my prostate as I told of these torments.

Archimedes listened anxiously to all this in a way that made me think he thought that I was somehow threatening him with these things. I tried to clarify what I saying by showing him another book on the subject; but though the book was in Spanish, I could tell he couldn't read. Instead, his eyes fastened on the logos of the many groups—trade unions, women's and students' organizations, guerrilla armies—that were opposed to the Guatemalan government. He turned the pages back and forth and studied those five-pointed stars, clasping hands, fists clutching AK-47s, sickles crossed by machetes. I attempted to explain some things about these groups, but it was hopeless. We heard a customer clomp into *Cosas*, so he left me, a confused and frightened look on his face. I figured I'd better learn better Spanish before I attempted such an "education" again.

And speaking of learning Spanish, a few days after Archimedes' visit a man who looked exactly like my old Spanish teacher in high school, middle-aged and jowly, dressed impeccably in a gray silk suit, came in. He began to browse so intently that I was too intimidated to speak to him at first. Finally he turned to me, and in an exigent baritone demanded to know if I was the owner of the store. I told him yes, and then he asked if it was "together" with the store down the hall.

"Oh, no, we're completely separate entities," I said. "Our businesses are very different. You see, they profit directly from exploitation, selling goods made by the poorest people of their country. I profit, when I profit at all, from books that in many cases expose that very exploitation."

The man glared at me in hard disbelief.

I watched him as he left. He paused at the display windows where Archimedes was arranging something. He spoke to him, and Archimedes crawled out of the space. The man placed his many-ringed hand on Archimedes' shoulder and Archimedes went down the street with the him. I thought it a little strange, but then shrugged it off as just another of the "Latino connections" my store would someday be famous for making.

A few days later, I again heard the man's baritone, rising to ever-more demanding heights, echoing down the hall, counterpointed by Ernesto's nervously high objections. An American voice was telling them both to shut up. Something big was happening down at *Cosas*. I hurried down to see.

The American wore the green uniform of the INS, the immigration agency, and there was another agent with him. The man in the suit stood with his ringed hand again on Archimedes' shoulder; Archimedes looked terrified. A fart of fear mingled with the copal.

Ernesto's long, pale fingers trembled as he handed some papers from his desk to the INS man, and his awkward elbow knocked over a basket of trouble dolls. The agent leafed through the papers, shaking his head mechanically.

The man in the silk suit grew impatient. "I have told you, this establishment is a front for the subversives," he insisted, glaring at me again.

He barked an order to Archimedes, and Archimedes pointed to a trunk.

"The propaganda is in there," the man told the agents. "That is where you will find their instructions."

The second agent opened the trunk. On top was Guatemalan clothing, bright with animal iconography. The agent took the clothing out, and at the bottom of the trunk were some yellowed newspapers adorned with some of the initials and logos I had shown Archimedes in the book.

"Terrorists," the man in the suit repeated. "They have links to the guerrillas. My government knows this."

"I don't know about that, sir," said the second agent.

The first agent kept looking over their papers, still shaking his head slowly. Ernesto's already sallow face began to take on an even deeper waxiness, and his pink-rimmed eyelids began to flutter.

In another moment, the agents were patting him and Susana down and handcuffing them.

"Why?" cried Susana. "What for you do this?" Her jet eyes fastened on me accusingly.

By the time the agents had finished locking Ernesto and Susana in their pasty green van, the man in the suit had Archimedes sequestered in his white car.

"To this one I give immunity," he said pompously, referring to Archimedes. The car had diplomatic plates.

One of the agents came back and locked up *Cosas*, and I was abandoned to the appalling silence.

It took me the rest of the afternoon to come to my senses and start calling human rights groups. I gave them as much information as I knew, hearing my voice distant and dead. They said they'd look into it.

I stayed close by the phone. A few days later a woman from one of the Catholic groups called back to say they had been unable to stop Ernesto's and Susana's deportation.

"We couldn't get political amnesty for them even though we could prove that Ernesto, at least, had been arrested and tortured by the Guatemalan government on at least one previous occasion," she said wearily. "The problem is, the State Department insists that most Central Americans in the U.S. illegally are what it calls economic, rather than political, refugees. In other words, they're just up here to work, according to State. Normally, though, the INS wouldn't send agents all the way to Taos just to bring in a couple of people, and the Dreyfuses probably knew that, but ironically ever since Governor Anaya declared New Mexico sanctuary for Central American refugees, the Feds have been doing these kinds of raids just to show who's boss. And that guy that came with them, the one with the car with the consular plates? We think we know who you're talking about, he works for the Guatemalan Consulate and he's bad news. He must have put a lot of pressure on the INS about the Dreyfuses. Unfortunately, if he's so convinced their store was some sort of 'front' for the guerrillas or whatever, he can make it real rough for them down there in Guatemala, too. You say you don't know what caused him to get suspicious about them?"

"No," I lied. "I don't."

I removed all the revolutionary literature from my window, and sooner rather than later, the Latins and the political people stopped coming to my store. Perhaps they had heard about what had happened, and rumors of my role in it. Who knows what kind of atrocious figure I had become in their eyes.

Meanwhile, I kept hoping against hope Ernesto's and Susana's disappearance would be a temporary thing, that one morning they would come trudging back in, foreheads straining against tump lines, backs heaped with gaudy bundles of new dream snakes, yarn paintings, grinning masks, that once again they would fling wide the doors of *Cosas* and I would have the chance to go down there and beg them to forgive my misunderstanding.

One late October day, as the clouds lay low and heavy over the Sangre de Cristos, I heard a van pull up outside, and my heart leaped for joy. But the van had U.S. Government plates: it was from Customs. As the first snow of the season began to swirl, two men started clearing everything out of *Cosas* and into the van. For a while I watched them; and then I locked my door, shutting myself in my store. I poured myself a big one and drank. Outside, the snow came down. I poured myself another, and another. I leaned against my bookshelves and closed my eyes and succumbed to a phantasmagoria of lurid images: soldiers burning villages, miserable Indians in their bright costume scattered on the steps of cathedrals, drunk as I, people with their thumbs tied behind their backs being "disappeared" by death squads. I fell to the floor and soon felt the burning pain of my own vomit in my nose and throat: the *ahogadito*.

Onslaught in the Upper Western Hemisphere

Jeffrey Lamar Coleman

*If this is not so, who can prove me false
and reduce my words to nothing?*   —*Job, 24:25*

Yesterday, a strong gust of wind
Blew through a rack of swollen cattle
Inside the butcher's shop
And carried downstream
An entire school of fish
Upside down, near the surface of the lake.

Today, air was finding its way home
When the first tender drops of rain fell.
Earth, again, mistook everything for blood
And moon was not allowed to appear.
Instead, a surrogate life
Carried us through the remaining hours.

Please, do not believe it all flashes before your eyes:
"Hey, it happened just like this in a dream once,
While father's ghost floated close to the ceiling."
No, that is not the way it happens at all.
It is more like finding one's self

Alone, midway through a sentence

Knowing once a period evolves,
That will mean the end
Of thought as we presently know it.
Yes—corridors, and an intricate sense or two:

That's the way it happens,
As if a glint of sun, bouncing
Off a butcher's shiny new blade.

Alone in Presence of Air

Jeffrey Lamar Coleman

for Denise

I am speaking today of bridges
And swollen voices: the way icicles constantly breed
In absence of words.

I am speaking of skeletons
We now consider broken bones,
Sockets of moons, canceled sunsets,
And the hungry stench of silence.

I am speaking of shafts separating sun from light:
Shapes of distance only flesh can consume.

I am speaking of evenings
Only memories now make love to.

I am speaking of air, fractured
And alone in presence of air.

Lately, I have grown away from bodies,
Bodies I once thought could be my own.

I have watched my selves disappear
Like phantoms sprawled and lost
In a vacuum of ancient whispers.

And I am no longer sure
If syllables we once embraced
Are asking to be held,
Or thrown away and forgotten.

Denise, today I can only speak,
And leave you nothing more than this:
Nothing more than a voice
We used to share. A voice
Now swollen, frozen
In the absence of our words.

Bus Station, Itea, Greece

Sören Johnson

In the bus station a woman raises
her voice. The ticket seller raises
his too. He charges what he
feels like and pockets the rest.

The voices rise, together and apart,
rise like seagulls chasing each other
for one piece of stale bread. First
one gull drops it, then another,
rising and subsiding above the harbor
until the bread is gone.

And then, gradually as springtime
in the far north, the voices settle.
A price has been agreed upon.
The bus arrives sweatily and the woman
comes out, black skirt and black sweater.
She walks slowly to the bus,
gripping her ticket in front of her.

The Waitress

Erika Lenz

The moment I stepped in the bar, I knew
it was over. One man leaned to another
and gave him a rose that would collect dust
on a windowsill. Then, yet another stranger
put his hands on my round belly and hummed.

And after the man in a wheelchair told me
how a white powder ate away his spine,
he laughed with the same looseness
that would creep over my Brent's mouth
on nights I sang at the Beacon—
the same ragged tilt to his lips

as when the comics were hit in the face
with fresh cream or Rohn tossed salads
in bowls on customer's heads.
This sudden replay of 20 years of my life
was simply too much to bear, I couldn't
stop myself, I told the man

every silly part of it: the cashier is an opera singer,
and every Friday the owner goes to prison
to visit the man who robbed him last winter.
My ankles have thickened to stalks
and I'm sure they have at least thirty rings
inside them. And the worst of it all:

My favorite pepper plants curl
around the speakers if I play them Bach.
Today, when my neighbor filmed them,
I saw their ecstacy in time-lapse, and—
here's where I paused—everything before,
the rumble of the organ in the Orpheum,
my father's home-grown peaches, the songs I sang
when I fed the chickens old greens at dusk—

it all forced me open like a newborn's head.
All my babies had the same desire, the same thick necks.
It used to be the doctor sewed me up
with fine knots and stitching, re-making me.
But this time, this baby, I'll have to tell him
there's no silk for this: those light-veined leaves

unfolding like tiny palms, their appetites
such a sensual rippling.
It's too much like coming home
and finding no one left to talk to, everywhere
this almost unseeable movement,
this wild life I no longer know how to live.

Drawing Blood

Cody Wasner

Like the hundreds of interns before him, John was late and tired as he dodged his way down the crowded hospital corridor, his long black pony tail flapping behind him. Unlike the others, however, he moved in the swift silence he had learned as a Nez Percé warrior. One could never stalk a bounding deer or catch an escaping rabbit unless one had learned to move. He used all his skills now, hesitating, weaving, darting to the left then the right, for even at 6:30 a.m. patients and staff filled the corridor. Underfunded and understaffed, County General had more patients than could be examined and more illness than could be treated. John, the first of his tribe to conquer medical school, was used to success, but at County there was no success, just survival. He wasn't sure he would survive.

He held his breath as he overtook the breakfast cart, a large steel box on wheels filled with breakfast trays. After four months of hospital cafeteria food, the least whiff of that metallic, antiseptic smell would send waves of nausea washing over him. It was the same type of conditioned nausea that his cancer patients felt when they walked into the chemotherapy room. He took a deep breath when he was safely past the cart. Side-stepping a stretcher, he bumped an orange-haired old lady clutching her IV pole. The collision jostled the old lady and set the two plastic bags swinging.

"You watch it, young man," she said shaking a crooked finger in front of his face.

"Sorry," he shouted over his shoulder as he raced on. He pointed to the overhead paging system. "Being paged."

"Doctor Carson, one East. Doctor Carson, one East," echoed the voice from the speaker.

The words "Doctor Carson" still sounded strange to him. He was proud of the word "Doctor," but "Carson" continued to grate on his nerves. It was a name forced on his family by the government because they couldn't spell or pronounce his Indian name. He had kept it in the white man's school, and of course it made life easier, even when he entered medicine. Now he was almost glad of his false name, glad that if he failed he would be failing as Dr. Carson, not Dr. Kaneehawanee. Besides, only his Grandfather would really care, and Grandfather was dead now. Of course, his Grandfather would say it was far worse to disappoint the dead than the living. Grandfather, who had a saying for every situation, had probably never failed. John even knew his

Grandfather's words for this situation: "For a warrior, persistence itself is victory." A hunter's words perhaps, but not those of a tired, discouraged intern. Grandfather would next look for a sign, a good omen. Like the rabbit darting across his path as he started an elk hunt. Maybe the orange-haired lady was a good omen, she did look a little like a dried up rabbit. The Infectious Disease ward was John's next hunt, and maybe it wasn't the hell that the other interns made it out to be. Maybe the stories of the users with endocarditis and the cancer patients with unpronounceable infections were just stories. Morning blood drawing, which was difficult on any rotation, was supposedly impossible on the Infectious Disease ward. The shooters, IV drug users, often got heart-valve infections, which required twelve weeks of antibiotics. Frequent monitoring meant weeks of searching for veins in addicts who had long ago junked up every usable site. The more he thought about it, the more he was sure he could use a good omen.

John arrived out of breath at the ID ward, where he was greeted by a wrinkled little nurse wearing a U.S. Army pin on her cap.

"You're late," she said barely moving her lips as she talked. She looked as thin and ill as most of his patients. Bones stuck out of everywhere against her uniform.

"Here's your list," she said.

She handed him a paper with ten names and a bag filled with needles, syringes, and yellow rubber tubing to use as a tourniquet. Wasting no time, John stumbled toward the first room, took a deep breath, and walked by the guard seated at the door. The guard, a common sight, meant a jail transfer. He stepped into the room which, with its faded pale green color and metal furniture, looked exactly like very other room he had been in. John figured the furniture was designed to be hosed down after each patient, and for some that was probably a good idea. He glanced at the name above the headboard—"Ms. Harrison"—then at the enormous woman resting on the bed. She must have weighed at least 300 pounds. but her ivory white skin and long blond ringlets seemed out of place on her gigantic head.

"Need a little sample of blood, Ms. Harrison," he said. His watch showed only forty minutes for ten draws. Fumbling through his pocket, he dumped the blood tubes and syringe on the bed. He stripped the tourniquet from his belt, wrapped it around her large arm and cinched it tight. The pressure should cause the veins to fill and give him a drawing site. He glanced at the lady, almost pretty in spite of her layers of fat, as she hunched over her breakfast tray, waiting to pounce. With long blond ringlets dangling down off her shoulders and the IV line running into her arm, she seemed like a Macy's parade balloon tethered to the hospital bed.

"Honey," she said, staring down at him through long dark eyelashes and a heavy layer of make-up, "you ain't got a chance." Her chubby hand picked up a roll smothered in raspberry jam and brought it within striking distance.

"No intern gets my blood first time," she said. She opened her jaw and the roll vanished.

"And call me Bambi, there ain't no Ms. Harrison here. If there ever was, I ate her long ago." She lowered her head and fluttered her eyelashes at him.

"Ah okay, ... Bambi," John said. His hands extended out in apology as he focused on the scattered scrambled eggs clinging to the plate. "I'll be back when you're finished." He gathered up his syringes, one by one, giving her time to acquiesce.

"Honey, no one can interrupt my eating. You just go right ahead." She nodded toward the tourniquet on her arm and settled her thick fingers on his forearm.

Her touch felt light, like a butterfly, and he was irritated by it, but he didn't know why. He reached for her bedside chart so that her hand would drop away. How gentle her touch was for someone whose arms might weigh more than he did.

"They got lucky on my leg two days ago," she said. She scooped up the last bite of eggs, spooned it in, then flung back the sheet with her left leg. Pointing with her fork, she circled an area on the top of her foot.

"Somewhere in here." She ignored the fact that her other ankle was fastened to the bed frame by steel handcuffs.

John eyed the cuffs. "You very dangerous?"

"Yeah, right. Like I could outrun anyone. Look, I sell a little stuff, you know, just so I can buy wholesale, and the whole goddamn government gets mad." She gave a mock pout and swung her curls in a fairly good imitation of Shirley Temple. "What's a little girl like me supposed to do?" Then she giggled and IV pole shook.

She watched him arrange the two needles and blood tubes at the end of the bed. On the night stand he placed a butterfly packet, his last hope if all else failed. A tiny needle with plastic wings affixed to a short length of tubing, it could enter small veins and remain there, stabilized by the plastic wings.

"Honey," she said, "you're gonna need more needles. Usually takes them an hour."

John frowned and tried not to act intimidated. He removed the tourniquet from her arm, which had failed to reveal any veins, and stretched it tightly around her elephantine leg. He examined several blue tracks, pressing them with his fingertips, but they didn't blanch. They were sclerosed veins, dry holes. A small tattooed star clung to the side of her ankle. A shooter would often hide a good vein in the middle of a tattoo so he searched it carefully but could find nothing. His back ached. He stood, stretched, then remembered his list and started again. He brushed his hand over her leg, searching for veins that could be felt but not seen. His fingers slid up and down little mounds of fat, searching for the telltale lump of a superficial vein, but he found nothing, nothing but porcelain-colored dough. Her skin felt soft and smooth like baby skin. Fat people had good skin. She was clean too and didn't smell.

Bambi mopped her plate with another roll and inhaled it. She glared at John, still fumbling around at her foot, and shook her blond curls. The entire bed rocked.

"Sweetie, you gotta pop them out. They ain't going to sit up and beg." She gestured toward her foot. "Tighten the tourniquet, it won't bite."

He cinched the tourniquet as tight as it would go and leaned over her foot. Her leg stiffened and lifted off the bed, twitching like some giant earthworm having a seizure. He jumped backward a good five feet. Her leg relaxed and dropped back on the bed. She laughed. Her blond curls bounced while the whole bed and most of the room shook.

"Just wanted to loosen you up, . . . honey" she said. A smile as broad as his shoulders floated across her face.

"Yeah, thanks." He couldn't help smiling, but he was ten minutes behind and didn't have time for any fat comedians. Picking a likely lump, he guided the needle through the skin. She didn't even flinch. He pulled back the syringe, . . . nothing.

"Shit," he said under his breath. He jammed the needle back in its plastic sheath, and pulled out a fresh one. He drew a deep breath and focused. The clang of the hallway breakfast carts faded. There were only his fingers, the needle, and this enormous leg. He jabbed again and caught a brief squirt of blood, then bubbles. He had lost the vacuum. He pulled out again and drew another breath. Scanning her calf, he saw a likely spot and slapped it with the back of his hand, hoping that the constrictive reaction would pop a vein to the surface.

"Sweetie," she said, with motherly tolerance, "that don't work on me. Too much padding." She rolled over toward the bedside table and punched the play button on a yellow plastic cassette player. "Honey, you need to relax," she said as a strong blues guitar wailed off in a direction he couldn't help but follow. The music carried him for a moment; then he forced himself back to his task. He focused on the clear plastic syringe with the #21 needle, angled at exactly forty-five degrees. His fingertips searched over the fat for a vein. A slight bulge caught his attention, and he took a blind stab. The blues guitar, now far in the distance, made a long slide, ending on a mournful E flat, punctuating his realization that this was another dry hole.

"Looks like we'll be here for a while, honey," she said, eyeing his jet black hair and olive skin. "You got a name? Qué pasa?"

It was the fourth time this week he'd been called Chicano. "I'm John, John Carson and I'm not Chicano," he said emphasizing the "not." He clenched his jaw and jabbed again. This time a just a tease of red blood shot into the syringe. "Damn," he said.

"Johnny Carson, huh. Your mama watch a lot of late night?" Her face turned serious. "Don't jive me, Johnny. What's your game? You ain't no Carson any more than I'm Audrey Hepburn." She brought her palm to her forehead in a mock theatrical pose.

"Hey, give me a break. You training for the FBI or something?" He glanced at her leg, which was beginning to turn dusky from the prolonged tourniquet. He pulled it off and the leg pinked up like a giant ham hock.

"Sorry, Bambi," he said. He was amazed that she hadn't complained. Tourniquet ischemia was painful. "Sorry," he said again and stroked the leg. He decided to try the right leg.

"Look, my name's Kaneehawanee. Okay? Nez Percé. When the government registered my father, the stupid clerk couldn't spell it. Gave him the fort's name. My uncle is named Meyers. Different fort, different name." He stared down at the old scarred linoleum, yellowed from years of poor cleaning.

"Hey, I'm sorry. So take the country back for all I care." She put her hands behind her head and stretched, revealing yards more of white soft flesh. "I like your real name, sounds exotic. You know, kinda macho."

"Yeah, right. Instead of 'Doc,' I'd have every patient in this funny farm calling me 'Chief' for the next year." He scanned the fresh leg, but there was not even a suggestion of a vein. His arms felt heavy, his legs ached. He thought of his grandfather, who would stand for hours in the icy creek water, his spear poised, waiting for the flash of a swimming steelhead. "Persistence is the mark of a real warrior," he always said. But, sometimes persistence could be fatal. Years of standing in the ice-cold water had damaged the old man's circulation. Never trusting modern medicine, even his grandson's, he refused surgery. His legs deteriorated and he died at home. Tenacity had gotten John through medical school, but he wondered now if he were like his grandfather and if the cold water of County General was slowly killing him.

John tightened the tourniquet and watched as a warrior, as his grandfather would have done. What seemed like hours passed, but no vein appeared. He poked desperately through a fold of skin where there was little fat. Nothing.

It was his last needle. "I'll be back," he said, slamming the syringe down on the table. He pointed at the ankle cuff fastened to the bedpost. "Don't . . . "

"I know, don't go away," she said, saluting him as he left. "Real original, Chief."

She has a great smile, he thought, even if she doesn't have one vein on her entire fat body. He stopped at the guard. "Hey, detective, unlock her cuff. I need that leg free." That wasn't exactly true, but he wanted the cuff off. The guard nodded and strolled into the room.

John hustled to the nursing station and stuffed a handful of needles into his pocket. His work sheet said there were two admissions waiting in the emergency room and a fever on ward three. Damn, he would be behind the entire day and up half the night. He ran, full speed down the hall, nodding to the guard as he entered.

"Heeere's Johnny," Bambi said with her pudgy arms outstretched.

John scowled. He was as tired of Johnny Carson jokes as he was of being called Chicano. This was a bad Fellini movie, a goddamn circus. She sat up, and as she lifted her massive flesh to a sitting position he saw a vein flash by at her elbow. She was staring him in the face now, her blue eyes clear and bright. Real nice eyes.

"Thanks for setting me free, Chief." She touched his arm.

"Sure. If I can't get your blood, we'll break you out of here." He grabbed a doughy arm, the one he thought had shown a vein. "Hope your arms are easier than your feet." He straightened her arm and secured the tourniquet, and in doing so knocked a get-well card off the nightstand. It was a large flowery card. He balanced it back on the table. "Get well Sis," it said in flawless calligraphy. Searching her arm, he couldn't help thinking of this "Sis." He saw her sitting by a swimming pool, Bambi's smile, Bambi's sparkling eyes but thin, almost anorectic. She was writing the get-well card and anguishing over her poor fallen sister.

He went back to the arm but there was no vein, nothing but fat: fat arm, fat hand, fat body. The vein had been only a wish, a trick of the lighting. As the blues guitar ended with a wailing A sharp, John gave up on the elbow and turned to the hand where he saw a small vein winding its way across her knuckle.

"This is a small one. You might feel it," he said. He cinched the tourniquet tight around her forearm and reached for the butterfly kit. "It's my last hope." He centered the small butterfly needle and hit dead on, but the vein was too small. It exploded into a small blue star burst. She closed her eyes but didn't say a word.

"Sorry," he said, applying pressure to the broken vein. "You'll have a nice bruise there tomorrow."

She was silent. Most addicts by now would be spitting or cussing. He gave a long sigh and slumped back into a chair. He propped his feet up on the corner of the bed and closed his eyes. He could hear his false name blaring over the loud speaker, paging him for the ER and the two admissions. He would quit. Grandfather died because he wouldn't quit. Drawing this blood did not matter. He leaned his head back and opened his eyes. Unconsciously, he began counting the tiny regular holes in the acoustic tile. He noticed that one entire tile was missing.

Bambi rolled off the side of the bed and closed the door. She waddled over to him in her circus tent of a gown and rested her hand on his forearm.

"Honey, it ain't that bad. Every user's got a vein, sometimes the junk is the only thing that keeps us alive. We all got a vein, you just got to find it." She leaned over and cranked up the foot of the bed so that the entire bed tilted toward the head. Lying down with her feet up and her head down, she turned her head to the side, exposing her neck.

"Chief, you tell anybody about this vein and you're dead. One night you'll find my fat little arms around your neck, squeezing whatever Indian blood you got left, out of you."

She took a deep breath and held it, bearing down like a woman in childbirth. From the pressure, the biggest external jugular vein he'd ever seen popped out between the folds of her neck and wormed its way up to her ear.

"Use a butterfly and hold pressure on it for five minutes when you're done, Chief. You blow this vein and you're one dead injun."

He positioned the butterfly and easily entered the gigantic vein. The reddish-blue blood shot into the syringe and splashed against the plunger. It felt warm against his hand, and he filled another syringe just to be sure. He pressed tight against the puncture wound. Her doughy skin felt soft under his hand. She had good skin. He wanted to compliment her on her skin, but he thought she would laugh, so he just stood there, his hand pressed against her neck, his fingers touching that good skin. When he became a grandfather, he would tell his Indian grandchildren of the lesson he had learned today. Using the same solemn voice his Grandfather had used he would say, "sometimes one succeeds by failure."

"Chief, you owe me one," she said, turning her head toward him. "And I'm collecting. Next time I hear your name over the loud speaker, it better be your real name. Now get the hell out of here. Answer your page before they think I ate you."

He leaned over and, like a monarch butterfly landing on a large flower, he settled his lips on her forehead. His lips felt cool against her warm soft skin. After a few moments he stood up and, like the monarchs that he had watched so many times on a warm summer morning in the forest, flapped his wings and moved on.

In America Yellow Is Still an Insult

Amy Uyematsu

1

I want to know why cowards are called yellow.
I've seen a few in my time with their ghostwhite skin.
Who named journalism yellow when it reached new lows,
and when did union traitors turn
into yellow dogs?

2

She says she won't wear amber, her birthstone.
Does its yellow remind her more of the shade of piss
than gold, a ripe lemon, or those famous fields of grain?
Is it the yellowish-green discoloration
in newborns endangered with jaundice?
Statistics back up her dislike,
yellow the least preferred of all
primary colors.

3

Immunize against
Hong Kong flu #5,
even more deadly
than last year's
Asian viral strain #44C,
microscopic infestations
of the latest yellow peril,
too many boatloads
and planefuls to stop.

Symptom:
Asians are the fastest growing
population in California.

                4

You can't even imagine being me, a yellow-skinned man.
Instant caricature.
Nameless slant-eyed enemy with kamikaze mentality.
Devious as Charlie Chan and his Karate Kid counterpart.
I'm Jerry Lewis on Saturday morning cartoons,
all buck-toothed and sing-song incomprehensible.
College nerd with no testosterone.
Grinning, squinting businessman
always dressed in the same dark suit and camera.
I'm cast as the voiceless boyfriend
who deserves to lose lovely Asian to big, brave Anglo,
I play the cowering eunuch
who stars in no woman's fantasies.
Just try to be a real yellow man in America
and know the legacy of insult.

In a Room Named Shimmer

Amy Uyematsu

—for Ann

The woman folds underwear
her husband's t-shirts still
warm from the dryer
filling a wicker basket.

It is night outside but a sheer
white light resides here
an attention her hands
devote to the ordinary.

She has just washed her sweater
carefully reshaped the wet wool
to the width of her thin shoulders
the two arms extended
a girl feeling them rise in the wind.

Next to the window she keeps
a painting from Mexico
two red snakes with grins
and wings while angels
dance over their heads.

There's an intention in each detail
some purpose assigned
the word shimmer on her east wall
closeby a small painted bird
resting almost unnoticed
until its wings begin to glisten
from some reflected light—
a life gleaned ever so slowly
each tiny glint more tremulous
and longing more insistent.

Nervous

John Couturier

You should never have stopped drinking.
I drive hours down I-95
through August's stewy air.

I swim through the parking lot's
melting asphalt
into cold corridors
through locked doors to find you
nailed to nervousness
eyes antsy and unfocused
voices telling disjointed "crazy" jokes
hair astray face gray-
whiskered fluttering hands
spilling coffee

You cried finding your wallet
empty of credit cards.
You tried to organize the inmates
against their therapy.

You should never
have stopped drinking;
sedated before
now your nerves have been cauterized
by their own fires.

BEYOND SCIENCE

C. John Graham

I walk in the kitchen.
A game show is on.
I say goodbye to vegetables.

The dog is under the carpet,
declining my invitation to get acquainted.
He doesn't know it's a different world,
remembers only parking meters and identical sets
of spotted cuttlefish in uniform schools.
Rules of grammar learned and obeyed.
A regular universe, the days
when the Ring Nebula was just a ring.

Now it's a supernova, dust and gas
blown everywhere, and what is left?
Blind acrobats, swarms of bees. Unexpected collisions
with disappointed barbers. Last minute decisions
involving red-shifted galaxies.
Maypoles unraveling, cracks in the sea.

But change is good. Like an atom,
most of me is empty space. I pass through walls,
hold conversations with risen saints. Orbit
a smooth white stone
while something receding in the distance
barks wildly in circles.

Cousins Once Removed

Pauline Mounsey

I tell you, there are onions that travel.
They move from one side of my garden
toward the other, leaving relatives
along the way, like the wagon train west
along the Oregon Trail through Nebraska,
scattering aunts and uncles and cousins,
leaving them to root in the soil,
small bulbs, green shoots reaching
toward clouds and blue sky,
growing the way onions grow,
then dropping to their knees
and reaching upward again,
a new crop of cousins, cousins
who have forgotten how
to pronounce my name, acting
like I am some kind of foreigner
without a home, a land.
This land is really mine, you know,
the corn rows and the wheat,
my new crop of onions.
Rain in spring, drought in
summer. I watch the crop,
hope it lives until harvest,
lives until geese take flight,
until I am left here with onions,
walking across this earth.

The One Who Fell

Mario Materassi

"Mister Osgood," said Paolo on the morning of his second day in America, "I would like very much if you would say to me how I can go to see the famous Empire State Building." He knew he should have addressed his "American father" by his first name. During the orientation program aboard ship, the Experiment in International Living counselors had urged all the foreign students to adopt this American custom. "Americans prefer a friendly, casual approach in human relations." Still, Paolo could not bring himself to call "Henry" this middle-aged giant he had known for less than twenty-four hours.

He now stood in the funny little kitchen with no doors and no window, respectfully waiting for Mr. Osgood to cool his coffee by sloshing it around in his mouth. Finally, Mr. Osgood swallowed. "You sure want to get a head start on your sightseeing, don't you?" He scratched the sole of his black-socked foot against the kitchen doorpost. "You're right. You've only got three weeks before school starts." He blew on his coffee again. "Honey!" he called, leaning back into the dining room and looking up at the incredibly low ceiling. "Honey, you tell Paolo how to get to 34th. I gotta rush." He wiggled his feet into his shoes, put down his cup and winked at Paolo. "Amy'll tell you. I gotta go—I'm late already. Take care."

Paolo waited in the kitchen for ten minutes, then ventured out. "Mrs. Osgood?" he said.

"Sure, come in. But please, Paolo, I told you: I'm Amy."

He moved up to the threshold of the master bedroom. Mrs. Osgood, her head magnified by a tight succession of gigantic pink curlers, her lilac nightgown stretched against the diverging buds of her knees, sat in the middle of the bed. A newspaper was laid out in front of her. She did not look up. "Come in," she said. "Come in."

"Excuse me."

"Boy," Mrs. Osgood said. "I don't know what we're going to do if this strike goes on much longer." she looked up. "Oh yes, sure. You want your directions. Two blocks south down to 86th. You take the downtown train to 72nd, get off and change to an express, on the same platform. Then you get off at 34th. That's your stop. O.K.?" She smiled at him. "I'd drive you down myself, but that would mean I'd lose my parking space. You had your breakfast?"

"Yes. Thank you very much, Mrs. Osgood. But," Paolo hesitated, "I would like to walk."

"Walk?" Mrs. Osgood stared at him. "What for?"

"Because I like to walk. I always walk in my city. It is good to walk."

"Oh," Mrs. Osgood said. She looked at him, her eyes wide open, her hands resting on her knees—a soft, mildly disconcerted Buddah. "Well, in that case, all you have to do is get to Broadway, turn right, and walk south for, let's see—fifty-four blocks, that's all."

Out on the stoop, he halted. His eyes half closed, he breathed in the early August breeze from the river. "I am in America," he said. His hand caressed the rough white stone of the balustrade. Then he looked up at the funny green bibs hanging from the roofs across the street, and at the long row of brown and white and grey steps leading up to the brown and white and grey doll houses with their paunchy façades and their guillotine windows. He breathed again, deeply. Then he slowly descended the five steps, glanced back at his new home, and started east.

The street was deserted. The long, long American cars were parked nose to tail in two solid lines. They had not moved since last night. Stubbornly clinging to their littered portion of gutter, they seemed to be the only rooted dwellers of the street.

At the corner, he almost bumped into an Air Force officer pushing a funny kind of baby carriage with a large canvas bag and one long handle. A green light blinked red in front of Paolo, and a huge, silent American car stopped noiselessly alongside him. He looked at the man behind the wheel as they both waited, then he recalled a counselor's words—"American's don't like to be stared at." He turned his eyes away.

On the opposite corner a young man also waited. A very small, almost brimless black hat was perched on top of his head. His black pants left his white socks visible.

They all waited. There was no traffic on the avenue, and Paolo had to fight the impulse to cross against the light. "Americans are fundamentally respectful of their laws." Finally, the light turned green.

The street was not so empty now. Two plump young women were coming his way, one in tight green pants, the other in tight pink pants. Big silver curlers stuck out from under thin scarves carefully chosen to match the pants. One of the women wheeled a wire basket loaded with paper bags and topped by a bunch of yellow plastic flowers.

He saw the outstretched leg the moment he passed the two women—the lace-less sneaker, the scaly, reddish ankle, the filthy pants leg ridged by the long thin bones. It lay at an odd angle to the body—a bundle of twisted limbs crumpled between the railing of a basement staircase and two empty garbage cans. The man's head rolled jerkily from side to side. Foam driveled through his stubble, trickled down the scrawny neck, on to the soiled T-shirt; it stained the sidewalk with a thin reticule of yellowish bubbles.

Paolo stared at the wide-open, unseeing eyes. He swallowed hard, then looked around. A woman was approaching, hugging a large bag of groceries to her fat breasts. Still bent over the moaning man, he waited for her, his eyes seeking hers. She walked slowly by, her hard gaze brushing past them.

"Madam—"

"The cops'll take care of him all right." She didn't even turn her head. He looked at her wide back as it waddled down the block and watched it disappear around the corner.

The street was empty now. Paolo jumped up and sprinted toward the great, noisy avenue. At the corner he caught a glimpse of his running image on the glass panes of a telephone booth, then he burst upon a flow of people, cars and busses. He stopped, looking for a policeman. There weren't any. He looked back down the street at the lump of rags lying on the sidewalk. A man followed his eyes. "Just a junkie," he said, and went on.

Paolo started running again. He darted among people, jumped clean over a litter of empty cartons in front of a supermarket, slalomed between the frozen glare of an old lady with pink hair and the sudden leap of a shrill white dog tied to a parking meter. At the next corner, while waiting for the light to change, he scanned the crowded avenue for a policeman. He raced down another block, and stopped breathless against a flow of people swelling out from an underground staircase.

He tried to talk to the newspaper seller, but people kept cutting in, grabbing a paper from a pile and exchanging coins that nobody even looked at. Finally, he touched the man's sleeve ("Americans don't like to be touched by strangers"). Panting, he said: "Please, sir, can you tell me where is a policeman?"

The man did not look at him but went on talking to himself. Paolo repeated his question. The man half-looked at him. "I jus' tolja, mistuh," he grumbled. "Right there in fron' uh yer eyes."

Again he had to wait for the light to change. Then he ran across the street but the officer was already moving slowly down the block. Paolo overtook him. "S-sir, s-sir!" he stammered, hopping sideways by the policeman under his cold scrutiny. He eagerly flung his arm in the opposite direction. "There is a man lying on the ground! He is very ill!"

The officer stopped, looking dubiously at him. "You a relative or something?" His stick leaped out of his huge red hand, and back in it again.

"No, no, I saw him. I was walking and I saw him. He is very grave!"

"All right."

They waited for the light to change. When it turned green, Paolo was already two steps ahead of the policeman. He stopped and looked at him, but it didn't make the other man walk any faster. Two or three times during their leisurely stroll Paolo said, "He looks very much ill," but the officer just kept looking at the traffic. They slowly walked around the litter of empty cartons in front of the supermarket.

At the corner, Paolo said, "It is here," and pointed to the man still lying on the sidewalk of the quiet, deserted street. Paolo thought he could hear the man's moans filter through\ the steady hum of the Broadway traffic.

The policeman nodded and went to a lamppost. He spirited a telephone out of a pea-green box, said something into it, and hung up. "They'll be here shortly," he said, looking at the light. "Thanks." he nodded to Paolo and began to stroll down the avenue again, his stick leaping rhythmically from his reddish wrist.

"But—," Paolo said. "But—"

On a cold, rainy day in February he saw the man again, lying on the ground in the crowded Vanderbilt Avenue exit of Grand Central. A trail of spittle glimmered dully on the lapels of his filthy army coat. His moans were just loud enough to make the hurrying crowd detour around his crumpled body. A few steps away, you couldn't hear him anymore.

Someone tugged at Paolo's sleeve—a middle-aged couple with cameras and heavy Western accents. He slowed down. "You're goin' the wrong direction, mister," he said. "You got to go back that way and get the crosstown shuttle. Then you take any IRT train down to 34th. That's the stop you want."

He hurried on down the long, resounding tunnel, once again in step with the crowd.

The Dissolution

Leilani Wright

after *The Book of Questions*

This mate of many years and I
are placed in separate but identical rooms:
mine is empty, except for a button
attached to the wall and a large
school clock that I know
is ticking away at the last sixty minutes
of one of our lives. I can save his

by alerting an authority beyond
this room with the pressure
of my thumb, but this gesture
would signal my own death.
The mate has this same option
to save me through self-sacrifice.

I wait. How long will he wait?
What must he be thinking?
this man whose soul I have slipped
again and again inside me.
If neither of us acts
within the hour,
we will both die instantly.

As for our child....
What would you do?
you who have all
the time in the world
to say goodbye.

Marks in My Skin

Craig M. Baehr

Mickey tells me she's been shopping
buying denim and velvet hats
funky ones with the bill in the front
and a flower
it helps keep the sun out of her eyes

i love you, baby
i love you, too
i'm dying
i know

my fist clenches tightly
sweat between my fingers
I am acutely aware
there's nothing they can do

the plastic tube sticks out of her side
bags keep fluid in her kidneys
funky hats hide the hair she lost to chemo
the stone that lies against her heart
grows from blood and wild cells
becoming stronger than her
feeding off her a piece at a time
the rest of living left to her will

I take off my shirt
look at the body I have grown into
between bone and muscle
the skin and the blood
that is half my mother's
part of hers is Mickey's

we prepare for this together
the succession of death
being born into our next roles
the earth reclaims her body
leaving a mark in my skin
the inheritance of blood and stories

Quick

Glenna Luschei

Everyone else sees the dead.
Why not me?
Why can't you appear
as suicides do
to those they left abruptly?
Sit on the edge of my bed!

You keep beneath the surface,
in my lungs.
Sink or swim,
I can't spit you out.

I've got you in the dead man's hold
but always underwater.
Come back just once.
Say, "This has to be quick."

Everyone else hears the dead.
Why not me?
"Death knocks, but does not enter,"
my grandmother said
and even though she was deaf
(her hearing aid looked like a church)
she heard the knocking,
heard the procession of ancestors
file by her grandmother's coffin
in the front door, out the back.

That time you dialed
into my dream
"I've got to take a trip
but the airport's closed."
I said, "I've got to hang up now
so someone else can take care of you."
Was it then I let you go?

Everyone else touches the dead.
I only wear the orchid you sent me.
When the postman rang
I wasn't home.
The orchid lay day after day in its box.
At last I lifted it out like a vampire.

The answer's obvious.
You completed your mission.
I don't need to be haunted.
We said goodbye.

My Father's Story

Troung Tran

so begins   *I'm tired* says the mouse
my father's story   of the cat   the mouse
of one chasing   the other running
one moves in   the other moves out
so it goes   my father's story
until one day   *I'm tired* says the mouse
I'm tired of chasing   my father retires

◆

My Father's Legacy

I thought by cremation
creation was possible
I could take your ashes
combined with clay
bring you back

in the shape of a vase
a set of tea cups
an old man
fishing at a corner
on my desk

Aunt Margie is Supposed to Die by Christmas

William B. Smith

I

It was always a ghost town,
not because it was abandoned, but
because one night it appeared
like a mushroom pushing up through pine needles
after a hard rain.

II

At the bottom of the long snake-road to Los Alamos
there is an adobe house under a gray cottonwood.
The scientists used to play bridge and drink coffee there
while waiting for mail and news of their families.

Scientists' barracks transformed to temporary housing
where Aunt Margie and Uncle Jerry live.
Maybe Oppenheimer lived in her house.
Probably not. Probably made a museum
where Oppenheimer slept.

III

Backyard opens to forest and canyon
where I used to play with Little Jerry.
There are steel suspension lines holding up a pipe
that bridges the canyon walls.

Little Jerry said that some drunk kid
jumped from there. Died.
Clutching onto the metallic rope,
I hear the wind whistling at my feet
and know it's true.

IV

I can't remember if I saw
barrels of nuclear waste down there,
or if I imagined it
when I heard the canyon was closed
for clean up.

V

She once told me,
"When we first moved in,
Big Jerry found this rope
hanging in the closet.
He had to cut it down."

Sleeping that night,
I saw a girl
leaping over my bed,
nightgown and noose trailing behind her.

VI

When I visited, I always looked at
Mike Huckabee's uniformed portrait.
Aunt Margie told me her oldest son had been
mildly retarded.

I could never tell.
I remember him laughing as he picked me up
and twirled me around so I could see
how the world would look when I was bigger.

VII

At Mike's funeral, after his suicide,
Little Jerry and I had to stay in the pews
while everyone else went to view the body.
We couldn't stop laughing. The only funny thing
was that we knew we weren't supposed to laugh.

VIII

One night we got a call that
Little Jerry had almost drowned.
The boat overturned and
he sank down through the gray waters.

He had given up when he saw
Jesus swimming toward him,
robes and all.
He doesn't remember getting back to the boat.

IX

Aunt Margie,
with her jet-black hair,
Oklahoman accent,
and liver spots on her hands like gloves,
is dying of cancer.

Why don't doctors tell her
she has a few more years
instead of a few more months?
She wants to live unitl Christmas
so Big Jerry won't be alone.

X

All these ghosts.

WET PAINT

Henry Rael, Jr.

On the corner of Locust and Grand, a tall clean-cut man is slouching with his weight resting on his knees. The sun reflects from the lenses of his round Lennon-style sunglasses so that any evidence of real eyes is burned away. Spending so much time outside in the radiance of this summer has seared his skin, endowed him with the red complexion that implies callused hands, years of white-trash bad luck. His arms are slack, hanging from his shoulders as if they would rather fall to the pavement. Balanced on his fingers, leaning against his thin, hollow chest, is a piece of cardboard; a simple message, written plainly: I WILL WORK FOR FOOD.

Ernie sees this man from 150 yards off and speeds up to try and catch the green light. Just as he pushes the accelerator, the light turns yellow so that it seems he is controlling the traffic signal from his car. Now he hits the brake. If he goes slow enough, the yellow will turn red and green again before he gets there. There is no way he can go slow enough, though, so he comes to a stop right next to the homeless man. By moving the tan Nissan Sentra forward just a few feet, he is able to use part of the vehicle's frame to obstruct his view of the burnt, stoic face.

Shifting his eyes to the left, Ernie can see just part of the sign, the ILL of WILL, the OOD of FOOD. The man's fingernails are visible where they curl around the piece of cardboard and they're not too dirty. Shifting his vision to the other direction, Ernie makes out the glow of green on the opposite signal and can see Marie sitting beside him, staring through the dirty windshield.

The sun has started early with its heat and the car is beginning to get uncomfortable. Ernie wants to roll down his window but he knows that if he does, the homeless man will think he's going to offer something. Marie is too quiet, her face pale and mean. On each side of him, it feels like the heat is being amplified, as though there are two huge mirrors forcing the sun into the car.

The signal changes from red to green with a quickness that implies a click and Ernie hits the gas. He forgets to release the clutch and the car roars as much as a four cylinder can while barely rolling forward. His foot comes off the clutch too fast and the Nissan jerks forward, the tires objecting with a quick squeal. He releases the gas and the vehicle dies in the middle of the intersection. Turning the key in the ignition, he restarts the engine, forces the gear shift lever into first (a raw grinding noise, loud) and turns the steering wheel so that he makes a left in a flurry of rubber, streaks of Big-O Tire marking the still-cool street.

Looking back over his left shoulder, he sees the homeless guy with his neck twisted, face irritated. The sun is gone from the lenses and his eyes look like they might be holes in the broken face. Ernie turns back to the windshield and then glances over at Marie. Nothing different, she just sighs like she wants to get this over with.

You know, we don't have to....

But the sentence comes from his mouth with reluctance and he feels like it collapses and dies right there on the floor between them, leaving a stagnant silence to intensify the warmth.

◆

The woman on the corner of Central and University doesn't have a sign, she just stands there and stares at the cars as they pass. She can't be more than three feet tall and so doesn't really need a piece of cardboard to ask for help; her oversized denim jacket says it all. The tan Nissan moves quickly past her, the driver keeping his eyes on the road, the passenger meeting the short woman's glance so absently that the woman turns and watches as the car disappears into the traffic up ahead.

Ernie makes his way around the other cars like they are all standing still. He is urgently drawn into the empty space created when a Buick changes lanes, and again when an old Firebird slows to make a right turn. But then he thinks again of his destination, of Marie sitting next to him, and he slows down and lets the Toyota truck to his left speed up and cut him off.

Central Avenue is already busy with half-asleep drivers and students crossing the street near the University. In front of a McDonald's, a short girl holds a sign, motions with her hand and yells at passing cars. CAR WASH, she says. KEEP KIDS OFF THE STREET.

There are few cars in the parking lot and he wonders if they might be early. The clock on the radio is blinking 7:00 sharp, though, and so he pulls into an empty space near the door of the office. Marie sighs again. He says:

We don't have to....

And again the words run unconvincingly from his mouth.

The door feels just like any cold door and he walks in first to hold it open for Marie. It's too late, however, when he realizes it swings in and he tries to keep it ajar while she enters and he feels she is struggling past him to get inside.

Just like a dentist's office, the air is cool and everything is clean. Two big skylights yawn in the high ceiling and a tall tropical plant seems uncomfortable in the corner it occupies. The only other people in the waiting room are an overweight woman and a girl sitting next to her. The receptionist doesn't smile, regards them with the same sort of expression the people who work at the Motor Vehicle Department wear: impatient and resigned. She talks to Marie, asks a few questions, has her sign some forms. Then, turning to Ernie, she says,

And that'll be Two Hundred and Seventy Five dollars. In advance.

She blinks twice, as if to prove she can, and then says:

We take Visa.

Thirteen Twenties, one Ten, one Five. He heaves the bills from his pocket and counts them out on the counter. The nurse blinks again, eyes the cash, then looks back at him like he did something wrong. He wonders if maybe he was supposed to sneak the money to her in a discreet way. But she scoops the paper up, jogs it into a sharp little pile, counts it again, and hits a button on a cash register.

Please have a seat. The nurse will be with you in a minute.

By the time he has turned, Marie is sitting across from the woman and the girl. Ernie eases himself onto the plastic padded cushion and cringes with all the noise it makes. When he is settled, he notices that the woman is staring at him: no malice, just blank, half-curious. Marie sighs. Sweat forms in a way he has never experienced, appearing in a single drop and running down the middle of his face so it stops on the tip of his nose and he jerks his hand up to wipe it off. There are travel magazines in front of him and he picks one up. Pictures of Hawaii, an unidentified beach, a cruise ship, happy people miles from home.

A door swings open and a thin woman passes into the room like she has practiced the motion a million times.

Marie. . . ?

She says it with a smile, speaking to every person in the room, maybe even to the plant. Marie stands and just before she disappears into the back room, turns; her face is tight, the nose wrinkled as if reacting to a bad smell. She moves past the nurse who smiles vaguely at Ernie and says in a low controlled voice:

It'll be about two and a half hours.

He counts the hours and a half off in his head: Seven, Eight, Nine, Nine-thirty. Nine-thirty is when he will have to be back.

Standing, he notices that the other two people in the room haven't moved at all. The girl's eyes are as they had been, half-closed, concentrating on her shoes. The older woman doesn't move except for her glance, which follows him as he makes his way to the door.

Ernie has been in the office for only a few minutes, but as he steps into the morning, it seems much hotter than it was before.

◆

There is a whole family that sits on the curb of the 12th Street off-ramp: Mom, Dad, two kids. The children (one boy, one girl), heads resting on their hands, look bored or tired. It's probably the biggest sign Ernie has seen and it says HOMELESS FAMILY, WILL WORK FOR FOOD, SHELTER, GOD BLESS, then, in smaller letters, PLEASE HELP. The father is reading a novel and the mother seems the only one paying any attention to the passing traffic. She notices Ernie's glance and raises her eyebrows hopefully. Looking quickly away, he hits the gas and speeds through a yellow light.

It is only eight o'clock and so he stops at a park near downtown. The trees are tall and full, casting thick shadows on the yellow grass. A man and woman are lying together at the base of a big sycamore, laughing and fondling each other. As he gets closer, Ernie can see that neither of them have much teeth, their smiles rotten and fleshy as they pinch and kiss, hands on cheeks and breasts and hips.

Leaning against an oak, Ernie notices how cool the darkness is and he breathes deeply, hoping the air will be as cool in his lungs as it is on his skin. But he can't taste the air at all. It flows in and out with the indifference of the passing motorists. There is a bench twenty feet from him and it looks brand new, reflecting points of light even from its place in the shade. He begins to make a move to go and sit, but his body doesn't respond.

They came here two weeks ago, him and Marie, walked beneath these very trees and had a nonsense discussion about the future. He had been quiet while she spoke and explained their options, formed two distinct lists, pros and cons.

The thing is, she said, we're just not ready, you know?

And she was trying to convince herself more than anyone else.

There's so much you want to do. We're so young. You'll resent me. You'll resent the kid. You'll resent everything.

The shadows had been longer then, the sun low on the west horizon. Now the morning is bright and Ernie can see every detail around him. Speaking out loud: Is this supposed to be a second chance?

But his voice, as it has been all day, is weak, and he feels silly for talking, saying words that make less sense to himself then they would to a random pedestrian.

As cars pass, the occupants look at him just long enough to make contact, then snap their heads forward as if they haven't seen a thing. They probably think I'm homeless, he thinks, smiling. They wonder where my sign is.

He walks over to the bench and sits. At first he doesn't notice but then feels like he is sliding with every shift of his weight. On the sidewalk in front of him a piece of paper winks at him, fluttered by a slight breeze. Moving to reach for it, he feels the stickiness as he peels his arm from the bench and he knows what the sign says even before he turns it over; red stripes on his clothes and hands and the paper hanging from his fingers: WET PAINT.

He wants to be mad and find the person who did this, but what would he do then? He stands and laughs until a few tears run down his neck and he realizes he is actually crying and he wipes his face, leaving thick oily red marks on his cheeks.

It's a new shirt and he takes it off, uses it to smear the paint from his face and hands. Back at the car, he takes off his pants and changes into some shorts and a muscle shirt he has left there since last week. He is tying the draw-string of the shorts when two bony fingers tap at his shoulder.

You got a quarter?

A short man, tan safari jacket zipped all the way up.

I got no home.

A grease-stained John Deere cap on his dirty head.

Why're you laughing for?

Ernie leans (collapses) against the side of his car.

This your car? What're you laughing about?

A dried leaf clings to the left leg of the man's new pants.

You laughing or crying?

Ernie meets the man's blue eyes and asks.

What did you choose?

Whadda you mean by that (offended)?

Did you ever choose to be what you are? Make a choice?

The man's outstretched hand turns into a fist and he extends his middle finger, holding it in Ernie's face.

Fuck you, O.K.? the man says, and backs off. He is thirty feet away when he looks back and yells over his shoulder,

At least I'm not stupid enough to go around sitting on wet benches.

Ernie opens his mouth to shout back but his voice again fails him. He squints with the brightness and half-shrugs. Speaking softly to the man who by now is almost fifteen yards away:

There was no sign, he says.

◆

On the curb in front of the clinic, a sheet of paper hanging brightly from her hand, Marie is sitting when Ernie pulls up at nine-fifteen. Her skin is pale, lighter than usual, glowing with the sun. Standing, she opens her own door and gets in the car before Ernie has come to a complete stop.

You changed your clothes, she says, noticing his muscle shirt.

The silence in the car is different now and at first Ernie attributes this to the open window, the air circulation. Then he notices that Marie is tapping her foot. She sighs. He doesn't know what to say, but then:

Do you want anything?

She shakes her head and her long straight hair doesn't seem to move. There is no make-up. That morning, she had dressed in comfortable, sweat pants and a T-shirt, just what she wore in high school whenever there was a big test.

Ernie's thoughts come to him in words, the way ideas appear in comic books, and he half-wonders if they are visible in bubbles around his head.

It's over, he thinks. Everything is different.

Marie sighs. The sun warms his hands on the steering wheel, shining through the dirtiness of the windshield as though there were no glass at all.

You want anything?

He faces her and she is watching a man yell at a pay-phone at Circle K.

No. Nothing.

He thinks: Everything is different.

You know, she begins to say.

What? What (patient)? And he taps her knee.

I couldn't do it.

What?

When she says nothing, he turns to her. She holds a piece of paper so he can read it. I COULDN'T DO IT, she has written there.

His right hand stays on her leg, his left controls the car.

Babe? she says.

The digital clock blinks, changing from nine-twenty-seven to nine-twenty-eight. On the corner of Broadway and Central, a nine-year-old kid wearing a Raiders cap waits for the DON'T WALK to change.

What happened to your hand? She touches the skin and her fingers are moist and cold.

Ernie glances for a moment at the red she is rubbing.

Wet paint, he says.

From the Terrace

Kathleen Spivack

On the terrace, a table.
Behind the table, two chairs.
Beyond the table, a wall.
Along the wall, white roses
spilling. And on the table,
two glasses.
Touching the glasses,
nervously, two hands.
Two right hands.
They turn the glasses.
They study the view.
The right hands do not belong
to the same person.
No, far from it.
Two left hands also rest
in two respective laps.

The owners of the hands
are silent in unison.
Beyond the table is
a terrace: no need
to converse. And beyond
the terrace, the wall
and the roses is a view:
a magnificent view.
There are mountains,
great pleats upon the
landscape, streaking
downward. There are tiny
villages, like play ones,
and yes, look, stretching
far below, a strip of sea.

Oh the relief of
that faraway azure,

finally. For the sea
absolves everyone
from speaking; gazing,
silent, as we do so,
outward toward that thin
cerulean void where even
sky-haze fades.

In the distance
an airplane lifts, a silent
silver dart. We sigh in
unison: we are both
travellers, meeting here,
parting past from future.
And now from this foreign height
we watch, as in a theatre,
nature going about
its day to day. Hands
lift glasses toward
pensive lips. Hands stop
and rest. Hands are
inexpressive and still,
like strangers
who, meeting, twitch
occasionally out of their
own private daydreams; or
like dogs asleep.
Like you and I
who meet this afternoon
on a flowered hotel terrace,
wondering how little
of our lives, untouched,
we might afford here,
looking downward,
nervous, past the table, wall,
and hillside to the outspread
vacant offering, the sea;
each right hand
clasping the left
hand of its owner.

After Summer

Kathleen Spivack

After summer
when we all come in
to be tucked
into shoeboxes
all scuffed and
sunny and exhausted,
it is as if we are trying out
our little graves.
The rain slants
on the windowpanes,
we don't know our lines
nor our silence either,
the rooms are unfamiliar,
dusty, and light
is already falling
too darkly upon
our faces. Late afternoons
we play dolls, dressing,
undressing, and there are no
lips dry on bare
skin, nor hands trying
out, nor textures. The sun
is cruelly bright,
prompting us, but then
falling away long
before we are ready.
It is too dark, too
early: intimations
of wanting-to-die
in the season. The
interior sets
with their dark windows
are stuffy enclosures

half sealed already,
and we put on thick costumes
as if for the first time,
as if at the dress rehearsal.

You Ask What I am Thinking About

Joanna Brooks

I remember and remember:
getting sexed off anti-porn tracts

hot from my parents' mailbox,
glossing all the good parts,

the pastor smiling over the postmark
(in the photo you can't see his hands);

prowling the neighbors' house,
smelling sex in disturbed sheets;

kissing Juli's brother in the junkyard,
black rot on oranges,

thick gravity draining their juice,
dogs licking their parts under the trampoline,

the green garden hoses tangling,
tongues out, everyone;

digging with trowels, strange worms,
the salty taste of concrete,

blood, pollens, marigold stink,
yellow fingers, contamination.

No untying this-that-there-now.
It's complicated business, is-ness.

A truce, entrenched between
"what was" and "what will be."

The me you hold is not the whole me;
I hold what you I know. I know

there is much else, unsaid surprises,
this salty solvent—compromises.

Tang, nasty, us.

The Dream of the White Bird

Lyn Lifshin

Ease is spliced,
but so raggedly
whatever it tries
to pass thru
tears it up like
shoes of victims
in a pile
50 years later
the leather still
smelling of their
feet and the
blood. Some
thing's flung back,
a banded bird, ringed
with coded figures,
something tagged
before it flies
flirting with an
other world it comes
back with clues
like a comb
from before
Christ, preserved
so well there
are still
lice on it

WATERMELON TREE

Joe Pitkin

In the grey morning
the man slips out the door
With a tower of cages
Loaded on his back, cages full
Of silent blue and yellow birds.

He thinks of his bedroom,
Where termites worm through the roof beams—
As he slept, bits of wood dropped
Like tiny dark mustard seeds
Onto his pillow, into his hair...

When he returns home for dinner,
He hasn't sold a single bird.
His two year old daughter is screaming,
She wants watermelon, not eggs!

Who raised this child
So badly, he thinks?

Suddenly, he envisions
His own, personal apocalypse:
The roof falls, breaking open
Every one of his cages,
And the watermelon seeds
His daughter swallowed
Take quick root in her belly—

As she breaks open,
A watermelon tree
Fills the ruins of the house.
In its branches,
Blue and yellow birds are singing.

Mental Chess

Thomas Swiss

Wanna try it? That's my brother, calling from the other bed,
asking me to play the game he's invented. He's king of the house,
my brother: older, quieter, doer of crosswords, reader of serious books...

Not that I cared or really thought much about him. Like my desk
piled high with baseball cards, the lump in my mattress,
the light that burned all night in the hall—he was just there,

a condition of childhood. Now, above the whir of the machine
that filtered pollen as it hummed all summer on our floor,
my brother was explaining the rules. It's like regular chess, he says,

except we do it in our heads. You know: no board.
No board? What was he saying? I could hardly play the real thing
during the day. But he had already begun, announcing his first move

in a voice so solemn I thought he was joking. And whatever
I'd managed to bring to mind vanished then, so that
when it was my turn, I was silent a long time until finally

my brother asked if I was sleeping. Not exactly, I thought,
lying in the dark, embarrassed and angry at myself. And at him
who nobody could touch. Like the woman I'd seen in the park that day,

bending to drink from a fountain while her boyfriend held the handle
But which figure was me? Which did I want to be? Even
with my eyes closed, I could tell what my brother was doing then—

turning off his reading light with a sock so he wouldn't get burned.

Walkie Talkie

Thomas Swiss

That tape-box from a talking doll, the Heath Kit stereo,
    anything with wires,
        tubes or transistors—

we loved and broke them all. But not our walkie talkies.
    Nights, in our rooms,
        we played at being deejays,

singing the Monkees, Beatles, Byrds. That's what
    I remember. And talking
        too much: our words spliced

with static, awash with others' in a stratosphere complete
    with coded beeps and buzzes. And when
        one of us grew sleepy,

both of us signed off: that's what I remember. And once,
    when I woke,
        I thought I heard you calling—

but was it *you* calling me across those big back yards?
    You, if I had answered then,
        who would have spoken

back again? Or was it only a local ham, or one from among
    the order of truckers
        whose nightly blabbing

I resented? Do you remember, neighbor? Dreamer
    or dreamed one, voice that held me
        at the glass: *Dave to Tom,*

it whispered, then hushed. *Dave to Tom,* it repeated.

Words In My Mouth, Don't Put Them; Ideas In My Head, Neither.

Robert Masterson

for SMS

I am divided, I find, when faced by window-slat shadows,
how this light is like that light buried there inside my head,
layer by layer through iron bars and glass
and a pattern of split bamboo and a roll of yellow paper,
how this light is modified by the filters through which it is passing.

A tangible slab of sunlight seems solid enough to hang from and
is a territory that dust may enter to become illuminated.
It apportions these spaces and helps to make them manageable,
sheds light on the objects with which these spaces will be filled:

> *this is a chenille bedspread*
> *this a pillow*
> *these are the walls*
> *this is a Rand McNally globe*
> *these are the small cars called Hot Wheels*
> *those are friendly stars that glow upon the ceiling*
> *these are the clothes to be worn to school this morning*

I wonder if that trinity of fruit trees will ever flourish,
if they will grow large enough to attract a Catholic vision—
a saint or two or three sitting quietly among strong blossoms.
I will always know that I will never get
the chance to see them, the trees, if they do.
There will always be other windows but
they will all be somewhere else.

A steady wash of river noise and lake
or of traffic or of air and thick pine,
a howl of electric wire out there and crooked moonlight,
are the constant markers for memories,
the things that will manage to make one place
pretty much like any other place.

◆

The boundary between the water and the atmosphere
is diminished by steam and the way it rises
from her shoulders,
from her arms,
from the tops of her breasts.

These are animal nights and we sit inside the water
and wait for dog sounds and night birds and
white-tail deer over the fences like rolling surf.
The part of the sky that glows, we call "stars"
and we begin to name them.

These are wicked times, we both agree, yet
so difficult to remember wickedness or how to be wicked.
It is so much softer than that,
an Egyptian posture and a pair of wings spread low over the pool,
a line of holy figures from old orchards turning back upon itself
 at the edge of the road and the horses murmur;
they grind their teeth and the big one, the appaloosa,
shifts his hips to move his right hind leg into an angle.

Our date was in the abandoned aquarium on the outskirts of town;
candles shed themselves upon us,
upon the scales of foreign fishes long dead,
upon the bones of performing penguins.
It was one of the best, that date,
and empty bleachers near the empty dolphin tanks made it more so.
We danced our newly learned dance-steps
in our new shoes and careful of the dust on the amphitheater floor;
and when we looked back to where we'd spun
we saw that we had surely been there.

Stealing Cars For Kelly Ashner

Robert Masterson

I started stealing cars when
I fell in love with Kelly Ashner.
She said she'd give me cash
for the cars I didn't want and
I believed her.
I've had plenty of relationships based on less,
based on geography (*we're both here*),
based on psychology (*we're both fucked up*),
based on physiology (*we're both only human*),
based on astronomy (*it's getting late; look at the stars*),
based on chemistry (*I wonder what was in that pill*),
based on anthropology (*we've both got opposable thumbs*).
Why not give economics a try?

I drive across the country finding good cars, clean cars, cars for Kelly's cash,
cars she would want to buy and the kind of cars that would make her father,
Ken Ashner himself, sit up and take notice and say
"I want to meet the young man who's bringing us these creampuffs.
By God, Kelly princess, bring me the man who brings me these cars!"
and that man was going to be me.

Through the midwest for heavy iron,
    the cameros from Lincoln
    the 442s from Ottumwa
    a charger and a roadrunner
the western states for pick-ups and ram-trucks and jacked-up, fattened up,
baby monster trucks,
and finally California for those low mileage foreigners
and most are leased anyway.
Snag a ride and drive straight through from anywhere to Albuquerque
and talk to Kelly.
I'll take the trade and tell her
"Okay, Kell. See you soon!"
and she'll say "Whoo-eee! I like the sound of that!"

McLean County Highway 39

Carrie Etter

The prairie wet with melted snow,
remains of dirt-covered drifts
in the ditch alongside the road.
There are no birds or cows
as the afternoon sky darkens
with clouds. The fierce wind
shakes the occasional oak and maple,
barren boughs waving like my sister's
thin arms wave at the county
airport, sending me off.
But it's Thursday and I
don't leave till Saturday.
Still I think about leaving as I cycle
past the barns, some dark red,
others rain-gray, always their paint peeling,
past the corn and soybean fields
between harvest and planting,
past the white clapboard houses
and dull aluminum silos.
Pushing against the howling wind,
I see my father on his bicycle
about ten yards ahead.
I can almost hear what he is saying.

Not Quite Auden

Carl Mayfield

A simple man
with a #9 wrench
in his back pocket
looks up from his plate
of rice & beans

I'm suddenly looking
into Auden's face—
the face he deserved
after ten thousand poems
& six million cigarettes

I look away
with the feeling
that I'm actually
witnessing the long afternoon
Auden realized he could have been
a diesel mechanic
for all the difference it makes

But I want to say
it does make a difference, kind sir
although I am not fool enough
to say it to this man
who has the decency
not to question why
I've looked at him twice

How can one destroyed face
move me so much?
A face long gone,
returning unannounced
with a brief stopover
in the Liberty Diner
to light another cigarette
to place the anonymous scowl
on someone else's talent
& not write another word

The Meaning of North Dallas

Bobby Byrd

Bernie learned the trick when he was working for his father at the family pawn shop on El Paso Street. On one of those polluted Thursday mornings in the hottest part of the desert summer, he tried to stick his key in the door, and it wouldn't go. He fiddled with it for maybe 15 minutes before he realized that somebody had fucked with the lock. A big black guy, a regular customer named Bobby, stood behind him with his arms wrapped around a small Sony 3-in-1 stereo system. Bobby was getting a kick out of watching Bernie fool with the lock and key. He didn't offer any help, just stood there enjoying the young pawn broker's frustration. When his fun got 15 minutes old, Bobby told Bernie the secret.

"Somebody super-glued you, my man."

"What?" Bernie asked.

"I said, Somebody super-glued you. Somebody got pissed off at you. You or your daddy. One or the other. It don't make a difference. Somebody who don't like pawn brokers, somebody who don't like the business you in. They come and squirted the super-glue in your door."

"Why would they do that?"

"They think you cheated them. That's how come."

"Bobby, we don't cheat nobody."

"You gotta tell them that. Not me. I'm standing here ready to do business. They probably watching right now. They smiling and laughing."

Bernie looked up and down the street. He saw people coming and going, he saw yesterday's trash being pushed around by a hot wind that was certainly undeserved so early in the morning, but he didn't see any customers. He saw only Sol Rubenstein sliding open the exotic Mexican wrought iron in front of his pawn shop. Bobby had a big grin on his face, two big gold capped teeth lighting up Bernie's nasty morning.

"You got to get yourself a locksmith, Bernie. Somebody knows how to use a torch. Me, I got to do my own business. Guess I'll wander on over to Sol's."

And with that, Bobby spun on his heel and, with enormous strides, headed across the street, the Number 10 Paisano Bus slammed on its brakes to miss him. Then Bernie had a hunch, he thought he understood.

"It was you, goddamnit," he yelled at Bobby's back. "It was you!"

Safely on the other side of the street, Bobby waved goodbye to Bernie with his huge coppery hand. Bobby was a good customer, so were his friends, so Bernie didn't say or do anything else. Bernie knew spilt milk when he saw it. It was probably his father's fault anyway. Everything bad or even confusing was his father's fault. Even the desert heat. Even El Paso.

That's what happens when you're a pawnbroker and you have a son. You get the blame. But Bernie's father wasn't a dummy. He taught his son to live and learn.

Always live and learn.

◆

Two months later Bernie moved to North Dallas. Bernie hated Dallas, North Dallas, but he liked the easy money. All he had to do was come up with smart-ass ideas so that his cousin Howard, the Born-Again Christian Jew who owned and operated Agape Enterprises, could make even more money.

Howard liked his cousin Bernie, even if he was still a Jew ("I'm not anything, I'm nothing, *nada* from El Paso," was Bernie's slick reply), because Bernie was the guy who had the idea of putting together the mailing addresses of all the famous and not-so-famous people in the United States. Bernie named the book *The World's Most Important Telephone Book*, but around the office he simply called it "The Good Book." In it a customer could find out where to send a letter to Michael Jordan, Newt Gingrich, the widows of Martin Luther King and Malcolm X, Tom Crews and Demi Moore, Larry Goodell, either George Bush, Walter Mosley, Joan MacIntosh, the lawyers of O.J. Simpson or O.J. Himself, Connie Chung, Paco Ignacio Taibo II, Noam Chomsky, William "The Fridge" Perry, Oliver North, or even Richard Baron and his brother Ho. Indeed, as the fancy big-busted lady in the advertisements said:

Anybody who is Anybody
(pause)
And then some more!

Agape Enterprises hustled it to sports nuts on ESPN, they did the same to media freaks on the entertainment channels, and to news addicts on Larry King, Rush Limbaugh and all the other talk shows on radio and television. It didn't matter if your politics were in right field, left field, or straight down the Pike, he Good Book had everything. Orders came pouring in at 25-bucks a pop, plus another $5 for postage and handling.

Bernie got $2 for each one. He made $14,696 the first two weeks of the operation. That means Agape Enterprises sold 7,348 copies of the Good Book in just 14 days.

"Holy Shit and Sweet Jesus," he declared every morning when he saw the orders piled on Elizabeth the secretary's desk.

Howard had tried to make Bernie be more Christian in his enthusiastic language, but it was of no use, although in the future he hoped and prayed that his wayward cousin would come around to see the truth of Christianity. Bernie, for his part, realized his impromptu vulgar outbursts didn't sit well with Howard, but he found it hard to mellow his choice of words. It was a habit built on 33 years of life. To make everything easier on Howard, he blamed his crude language on his father, an excuse that Howard found acceptable. Howard had never liked his Uncle Moses because he thought pawn shops to be a disreputable way of making money. And he hated El Paso. To him it was just a dirty city where too many people didn't even know how to speak English and, besides, there were too many Catholics.

All of this is not to say that Bernie didn't like Howard. He did. He even admired his cousin. But he could not take seriously any of his codes of Christian conduct. What Bernie cared about was, first, the quick money, followed quickly by Elizabeth's nice red lips and, of course, her ample breasts which she hid demurely behind conservative business suits. Bernie hoped, even prayed, that Elizabeth dressed North Dallas Baptist only for Howard's benefit. He knew that Howard had hired her because he knew her father, a deacon at the church he attended, a move which was both good religion and good business. Elizabeth, in turn, liked the generous salary that Howard paid her once a week. If Howard wanted her to dress like a virgin (this was Bernie's assumption), then she would dress like a virgin. She was no dummy.

Bernie also played, within the bounds of his personality, the part that Howard wished him to play. He was no dummy either. He did not want to tump over his own apple cart. The money was simply too good.

◆

One morning Bernie had this idea of manufacturing condoms that looked like Subcommandante Marcos, the famous guerrilla leader of the *Zapatistas* in the State of Chiapas, Mexico. Marcos had become famous overnight because he wore a ski mask during all of his interviews, and the press, hungry for an exciting, even intelligent, new international hero, loved the guy. The idea popped into Bernie's head while he was sitting on the toilet reading *Newsweek*. He had many of his ideas while sitting on the toilet. He was fond of pointing out to Howard that Martin Luther himself had received his own vision of Christ while crouched over a similar throne.

On this particular morning, he read a long tongue-in-cheek article (the appropriate *Newsweek* style for information discussing Mexico with its curious folkways, especially in regards to sex) detailing how condoms tipped with the image of Marcos in his celebrated ski mask were selling like hot cakes in Mexico.

Voila!

With the right advertising, Bernie figured that Marcos-tipped condoms would do the same thing in the United States, what with the AIDS scare, the blossoming of condom boutiques in all the hip neighborhoods throughout the country, plus our continual love affair with armed revolution. As soon as he got off the pot and carefully washed his hands, Bernie sat down at his computer and typed up a four page, single-spaced memo to his cousin Howard explaining the why's and wherefore's of his project, plus the minimum costs and the incredible profits to be made. The memo cost him six long hours of his time, several long and elaborate modem searches on CompuServe, and a pot of his most expensive Columbian coffee. When he was done, he hurried over to the office where he dumped the project into Howard's In-Basket.

"Elizabeth," he told her, "we're gonna make a ton of money in service to the Great God of Love!"

Elizabeth blushed and smiled, then straightened her tweed business jacket which hid her lovely self. For a moment, Bernie meditated upon what the jacket actually did hide, then he disappeared into his small office where he waited patiently for his cousin to buzz him. To pass the time he read a James Ellroy novel that had Walt Disney as a bad guy in the mean-spirited kingdom of 1950s Los Angeles. Bernie lost himself until 4:30 in the afternoon when Howard called him into his elegant office that looked over the repetitive condominiums of North Dallas. Howard's face, which never looked comfortable in the first place, was stuck on top of his $500 suit and $35 tie like a beet with reading glasses.

Oh oh, Bernie thought.

"Aren't you well?" he asked Howard.

Howard didn't say a word. Instead, he simply looked at the ceiling, breathing hard while his cousin could only watch and wait. Finally, Howard composed himself enough so that he could return Bernie's stare.

"I am a Christian man, a man of the Baptist faith," is what he said.

"Yes?" Bernie asked, realizing immediately that something was amiss. Again he waited while Howard looked at the ceiling and breathed the air like he had just run three miles in the worst of Dallas's ugly swampy heat. Bernie soon grasped that he was praying. Oh oh, he thought again. Five minutes passed while Howard continued to breathe and pray. Then he looked at his cousin.

"I will make this short and sweet, then I will ask you to leave the office for a week while I think about our relationship, business and otherwise."

"What?" Bernie asked.

"Listen, here, Bernard," Howard said, his voice tinged with anger and disappointment, like he was talking to a precocious but wayward child. "As a Christian man, I do not believe in anything which will give license to sexual promiscuity."

"But . . . ," Bernie tried to intervene with his arguments about the devastation of the AIDS epidemic as well as the amount of money there was to be made from selling hip novelty items like condoms. He, of course, understood that Howard, like himself, enjoyed making money. Howard raised his finger to his lips so that Bernie would shut up. Which is what Bernie did.

Howard continued in a solemn voice. "Nor do I condone—how shall I say?—armed revolution by Godless communists." And without pausing again, he added, "Now you may leave my office. I don't want to see you again for at least a week."

Having ordered the final punishment, he went back to his breathing and praying. Bernie left without saying another word. He didn't even say goodbye to Elizabeth as he left, but he was careful not to slam any doors. Howard hated anybody who slammed doors.

It was weird to be exiled from his office for a week. At first, he was extremely angry. He hated his cousin Howard for treating him like a child, he hated Christianity, especially North Dallas Baptist Christianity, for making Howard (once a good and normal non-observing Jew, just like himself) lose the joy of making a living, he hated not having the opportunity of chitchatting with Elizabeth every day and of daydreaming about her underclothes, he hated not having anything to think about, and, most importantly, he hated being bored. But then, on the third day of his exile, he realized, while sitting on the pot and reading the *Dallas Morning News*, that he was on vacation. Didn't he continue to make $2 each and every time some dunce picked up the phone, American Express card in hand, and ordered *The World's Most Important Telephone Book*? It wasn't so much Howard being the fool. It was him, Bernie. He was being a fool. He should enjoy himself. He started immediately making the effort to enjoy himself. He called his old friends in El Paso. They talked together, they laughed together, and Howard invited each and every one to come visit in Dallas, although he knew that they never would. They hated Dallas. He even called some old girl friends from El Paso. He apologized to them for being such an asshole all his life, he told them that he could understand their point of view, and he wished they would come and visit.

"Please, pretty please," he even said to Arlene, the one woman he still loved. Maybe, if she had given him the chance, he might have even married her, but she didn't. She wanted her own life.

"Maybe in August," Arlene told him.

"You're still a liar and a bitch," he said into the phone after she hung up. And so ended his first few hours of trying to enjoy himself on his unexpected vacation.

Next, he decided to go to the afternoon movies, something he hadn't done for years. He saw *Zen and Sex* which only made him horny. When he exited the darkness of make-believe, the Dallas twilight clung to him like a moist scab. He went to a sushi place to lift his spirits. The raw fish was delicious, the saki delightful, but the experience had left him even more horny. That's why his next stop was a singles bar near his apartment. He had the faint outside hope that perhaps he could find a cure for his sorrow.

The place was called Happy Mud, and it too filled itself with darkness and make-believe. He found there a beautiful woman in tight white pants who flirted with him while delivering huge vodka martinis. She even bent down from time to time in the performance of her duty so that Bernie could gaze at the mounds of pleasure inside her shiny red blouse. He got so drunk he could hardly walk to the bathroom. Around 11 White Pants suddenly became a business woman. She checked his wallet for sufficient funds, then called a cab which delivered him bodily to the front door of his apartment. On the fourth day of his exile, Bernie awoke with a horrible hangover and a desire to go back to work.

He spent that whole day enjoying the fruits of his anguish. He finished the James Ellroy book where Walt Disney, thank God, received the ugly death he so richly deserved. During the morning he drank the expensive Colombian coffee, during the afternoon he drank only water, and that evening, he slugged down several vodka martinis which lifted his spirits considerably. After a late dinner of a poached filet of sole, salad and potato bathed in butter and sour cream (Bernie always treated himself nice, no matter the occasion), followed by a quick shot of reality, sports and weather on the 10 o'clock news, he drove over to a nearby Walgreen's where he bought himself a small squeeze bottle of Super Glue.

✦

Elizabeth was glad to hear Bernie's voice. She even confessed that she missed him, and she thought that Howard missed him also.

"Yeah?" Bernie asked.

"He's not even here today. He called me before I left my apartment," she purred. "He said he was sick. And he's never been sick, not as long as I've been here."

"Yeah?" Bernie asked again.

He was feeling better already. They talked some more. Elizabeth informed him that he had made exactly $2,814 during his absence. She had been keeping track for him, she knew that the figures made him happy.

"Yeah?"

There was a long pause.

"I didn't even wear my suit today. It's so hot. And Howard's not going to be here anyway. I just wore my jeans and a comfortable blouse."

"Yeah?" Bernie asked one last time.

"Bernie," she said, "today is the last day. You can come back tomorrow. Isn't that right?"

"I hope so," Bernie said.

◆

He set the alarm for five thirty, but he was already up 20 minutes before the thing went off. First off he took his morning dump, he showered and shaved, then he wandered over to Denny's to join all the other legions of good Americans on their way to work. He felt a part of something much bigger than himself. Of course, he wasn't on his way to work just yet. He was just getting ready.

Food was of primary importance for the day in front of him. He ate a big breakfast, a three-egg mushroom and spinach omelette with toast and hashed brown potatoes, and he drank only two cups of coffee. The next order of business was the *Dallas Morning News* which he read from cover to cover for the first time since his exile began. This was almost as important as food for any young entrepreneur who sometimes ended up exchanging gossip about the news with people like Howard or Elizabeth. It was that morning somewhere between 8:00 and 8:30, when he was walking back to his apartment, that Bernie decided that O.J. Simpson did in fact kill his ex-wife Nicole and that Bulgaria, as much as he enjoyed their blue collar spirit, would lose to Italy in the semi-finals of the World Cup. Such decisions always lifted his spirits, and he changed into his chosen apparel with a definite joy.

When Bernie strolled into the office building at exactly 9:33 (he liked the luck that those numbers promised), he had on his best suit, a dark gray $225 double-breasted jobbie that he set off with a light blue pin-striped shirt and a wildly red-hot abstract $15 Jerry Garcia tie. His hair had been coiffed the evening before, his nails manicured, a new experience for him. He looked perfect, he thought, as well he should. When he stepped off the elevator and turned toward the northwest corner suite of offices which was Agape Enterprises, Bernie was delighted to see Howard and Elizabeth waiting outside the office door.

But they weren't exactly waiting for him. They were staring at the door, and Howard was shaking the door knob. Elizabeth stood behind her boss, peering over his shoulder and every few seconds she made a soft mewing sound. She sounded like a hungry cat. Bernie walked up behind them and cleared his throat like they do in the movies. Elizabeth turned around and gave him a big smile of moistened red lipstick that made promises that he certainly hadn't expected. He was glad to see her too, but he was somewhat surprised to see her in a skirt that crept two nice inches above her kneecap and a white cashmere blouse that displayed her wonderful breasts. He thought it safe to try out a hug and a quick buss on the cheek. She responded warmly.

Bernie then turned, with some anxiety, to say hello to his cousin Howard who was kicking at the office door and who had not even noticed Bernie's arrival as yet.

"Hello, Howard. I'm back."

Howard turned around, and as he did so, Bernie was able to witness the metamorphosis of his cousin's ugly frown as it refashioned itself, like magic, into a wide grin.

"Bernie!" Howard almost shouted. "Cousin Bernie. I've missed you." He grabbed Bernie by the shoulders and gave him an awkward, but warm and manly, hug. Bernie returned the embrace.

"Yeah?" Bernie asked.

"Yeah," Howard said.

"Me too," Bernie said. They stood there for a few seconds in each other's arms until they couldn't stand it anymore. Howard was even blushing.

"What's wrong with the door?" Bernie asked him.

"I can't get the fucking thing open." Howard stumbled over the first profane word he had spoken in well over a year. He blushed some more. Bernie looked at him and smiled.

"Here, let me see what I can do," he said, and the two cousins turned to confront the mystery of the door.

THE ONE-HANDED MARY

Enid Osborn

1

Give me your hand, Mary
Your hand is the best part of you
The unpierced hand
peace and compassion flowing
Give me your hand
where it comes off at the wrist
where it cracks inside the fabric of your sleeve
old-timey mannequin that you are

I have longed to stroke your small palm
to feel it resting on my hairy crown
not for an instant, but for a little while
until I feel better

Mary, give me your hand
I will tie it onto my head
with a bright scarf, something festive
I will wear it there for days
It will make me feel like laughing
I will wear it to the grocery store
and to sweep my rooms
and I will wear it to morning mass
Wear it right back into the mother church
and right up the aisle
to bob a curtsy at your feet
No one will know our secret
only think
That woman
 Her scarf is too bright
she laughs in church her curtsy is too small
But you smiling down
with a twinkle in your painted eye

2

At night I take your hand from my head
With a sigh, I remove it
with the same care my grandmother used
to take the long pins from her small felt cap
By now your hand has molded neatly to my crown
and my hair curls lovingly around your fingers
Carefully I remove your hand
and lay it on the clean linen beside my pillow
I say my prayers, kiss your hand
turn out the light
and lie in darkness
Sleep won't come
I feel a small loneliness beside me
your fingers reaching in the dark
I pull your hand close, cuddle it to my face
Lick it to sleep like a kitten
Tuck it into my nightshirt, against my warm belly

3

We spend long hours in the garden together
I set your hand
in the fork of the fern, the John's wort, the messy rosemary
You hang on without effort and I forget to worry
One day I cannot find where I laid my little digging spade
Absently I snatch your hand from its place
and bury your fingers deep in the damp earth
We plant seedlings for the new moon
They grow so well, we do this for each new moon
of fish and bull and snake and crab and virgin
The herb garden has never been so fragrant

The paint begins to chip from your fingertips
where they repeatedly knock
against the little rocks in the humus
where the worms brush by
where the water wants in
Beneath the paint, the clay of your hand is brown

4

In time your hand is truly at home here
I know this because I cannot find it
Rather, I forget to look for it
Or, I look and I don't see it

Your hand is lost among the clutter
on my rustic table of weeds and wood

Your fingers poke out from under
the sewing scraps

You are dug into the pocket of my old coat
jingling small change

You are holding the portable telephone

5

This is how we celebrate the seasons:

I fill your hand with pink rose petals
I fill your hand with tiny blue eggshells
I fill your hand with sea water tears
I fill your hand with sun-warmed sand
I fill your hand with honey from the tree
I fill your hand with shining beetle wings
I forget to fill it
I fill your hand with loquat seeds
I fill your hand with the blood of the rooster
I fill your hand with a sycamore leaf
I fill your hand with the soft body of a drowned bee
I fill your hand with December snow.

6

Meanwhile, back at the church
Your miracles multiply
And the snow melts, another miracle
People cover your body with shining milagros
They march up the aisle to you on their knees
They call you "The One-Handed Mary"
They make you resplendent with candles of asking
They speak of your losses: first your son, then your hand

They attribute your powers to the pain and the sacrifices
But you and I know, (we know, don't we, Mary)
It is what we are given
that we have to give
The nature of kindness
in the happy hand.

The Almanac is Predicting a Harsh Winter

Jennifer Miller

Gary died in the snow. Should I mention her harelip?
Women aren't saving enough for retirement.
My father says, "You can't have everything
you want."

When I was little I remember Auntie Carol
had hair dye in her ears. I thought it was diabetes.
Last week. Her harelip. Jesus is the answer.
Retirement. There is no such thing
as a dumb question. My sister's been dreaming
of midgets. The almanac is predicting. Everything
you want.

In Mexico they take two hour lunch breaks.
My best friend just had twins. Midgets.
It is a good thing to struggle. It makes you strong.
Hair dye in my. Dumb question.
My grandparents had a black maid
who was afraid of lightning. I thought it was.
There is no such thing.

My father says, "Beef and peanut-butter
make the world go 'round." In Mexico
they take. Beef and. Jesus.
My father says, "Things could be a lot worse.
Consider yourself lucky." Dreaming. Yourself lucky.
Lightning. Gary. The answer.
The almanac is predicting a harsh winter.

The Clock Inside My Father Breaks

Alexis K. Rotella

and the man in the white coat
who usually resets it is away on vacation

another clock maker is appointed
to my father's case who also goes out of town
to leave another fixer of timepieces in charge

but by then my father's clock is too slow
to rewind its spring has sprung and they don't
make them anymore

my father's inner jewels are dimming
planets from another galaxy are sending him light.

Run For Ice

Alexis K. Rotella

The long beak
of a hummingbird
drills into
my mother's brow
and she walks out
the cellar door.

Run for ice
she yells to Dad
I've been stabbed.

Another September Song

Glen Sorestad

We bend as the sun splashes the garden
in old greens and yellows to pluck
cucumbers. A September morning. Crisp
faded vines crinkled with autumn.

This is our last cucumber day, we say,
and uncover the shy fruit, small or large,
from their stiff-leafed sanctuary.
We live little to the coming frost.

Already the sun flies further south
and sweater-clad dawn comes later.
We will jar these fruits of summer
for the feasts of winter. Let frost

come as it will. We both know well
that frost comes hand in hand
with fire: as green walks with gold.
Heads in the sun, our feet are on earth.

Streetlights

Jenny Goldberg

The darkness slips from the sky. I feel it.
People squat by fires under streetlights. I know them.
The predawn strays through our window.
I see the rise and fall of your big belly.
I shiver under your wrinkled arm.
You lie beside me drunk.
I hear the snow shifting on the roof.
When the sun sneaks over the East River,
I will turn sixteen.
Tomorrow the roof of our loft will leak,
and your daughter will be gone.

Rights

Iqbal Pittalwala

I'm sitting alone on a bench in the local mall as I often do, reading a brand-new short-story collection by Joyce Carol Oates—if you haven't heard of her you should consider shooting yourself soon— because I want to keep up with her writing and have been improving my vocabulary by studying her work, when suddenly, as I flip the page and come to the final paragraph of a suspenseful story, I see on the opposite bench a woman leaning into a perambulator (some months ago, I'd have said 'baby carriage') blowing bubbles through a long, looped wire. She's aiming these bubbles at a baby trapped somewhere in the perambulator, I figure. The helpless baby, I think. So I put my book down on my lap, cup my hand by my mouth and ask the woman to stop the bubble-blowing at once. She looks at me like I'm some doggy-doo just landed in the mall from planet Pluto. She ignores me and stirs the liquid in the bottle she holds in her hand. She brings the looped wire to her puckered mouth and produces another parade of bubbles that proceeds toward the baby who, poor thing, hasn't the words to protest yet. I snap the book shut real hard so that it sounds like a gun-shot. I spring to my feet and walk up to her. Now she sits back. She's alarmed, I can tell, but scaring her wasn't the idea, I swear. I say politely, "Madam, I implore you not to blow any more bubbles at Junior here." She stares at me for a few seconds, batting her eyelids, and says, "Get lost, asshole." This in front of Junior, who is looking at me with his big glassy eyes, his plump arms waving in the air, urging me to reach down and rescue him from further bubble-onslaughts. I stand there smiling at him and we're communicating without words, building a rapport between us, a solidarity, the way guys easily do, when, out of the blue, the woman says to me, "Get the fuck out of here." So I click my shoes together, stick my chest out and walk away from her and Junior. I walk only a few steps when I look quickly over my shoulder and catch her dispatching bubbles in Junior's direction again. I wheel around and rush over to poke them with my finger—pop! pop! pop!—before any can get to Junior's face. "You *ass*—hole!" she says softly, staring in disbelief at where the bubbles were. She rises and I tell her—politely, mind you—that I'm not going to just sit around and watch Junior suffer 'incessant bombardments of glutinous, lathery bubbles.' I can tell from her parted lips that she's impressed with my vocabulary, so I ask, "How would you like it, madam, if I bounced a balloon repeatedly on your nose?" I thought I was pretty creative but she isn't awed and takes to grunting and breathing fast like something about to spin and shoot through the roof. She clenches her jaws, and looks around for mall security (she doesn't know I'm a regular bench-reader at the mall, that everyone here knows me well) and when she spots no one in uniform, she tells me, with her fists slammed into her sides, to go fuck myself somewhere. "Mind your language, please," I tell her because I'm concerned about my buddy Junior hearing her profanities and growing up, you know, to be foul-mouthed like her. "I understand your parents were the liberal-minded sort," I tell her, maintaining a calm tone. She turns around to grab her bottle of detergent or whatever they fill it with and she tosses the greenish-blue liquid toward my face as if it's *my* mouth that could use some suds! She misses because I anticipate her move and step back at the last moment. The liquid splashes instead on my hands and on Ms. Oates's book, which I'd instinctively pulled up to my chest, the way I do whenever her writing touches my heart. So now the book's wet and this liquid's streaming down the back cover, in fact, over Ms. Oates's face shown there in black and white, and I'm pissed. I mean I'm really, *really* pissed. "This, you incorrigible imbecile, is Joyce Carol Oates," I tell the woman. "What?" she says, grimacing. "Who gives a shit? Go to hell, goddammit. Both of you." Now that's the last straw. I'm shaking with rage. I'm snorting. Somehow, I manage to open the book to the page I was reading and thrust the book toward her face. "Read," I tell her, stepping forward. "Read, read, read." She moves back, baffled. "I was on the last page of— this phenomenal story," I go on, sifting through my mind for better words, my voice not so calm anymore. "Peruse Ms. Oates and redeem yourself." She screws up her face, shakes her head and says, "You crazy son of a bitch." She lunges toward me. She pushes the book against my chest. Some folks gather around to watch us. Somewhere there's some giggling too. I take the book and slam it hard against her face. She cries out, feels her mouth and nose, and reaches for the book. Her coppery hair flies here and there. She grabs a hold of the book but, of course, I don't let go. She pulls, I pull, she pulls, I pull, and then—you've guessed it—it happens. A page tears. We stop to stare at the book in our hands. The last page of the story is gone. It sprouts like a blade from between her fingers. That's it. THAT IS IT, I tell myself. The tug-of-war resumes. Back and forth, back and forth. Soon there are all these bubbles floating in the air and sliding down the book's glossy jacket, and as we go on shuttling Ms. Oates's collection between us, these bubbles increase in number and march down our hands as though to the music playing in the mall and one of these bubbles, moderately sized, drifts menacingly toward Junior so that now I'm wrestling with two things at once: one, get her to release the book *and* the torn page that's fluttering like a flag in her hand, and two, explode the bubble before it makes it to Junior in the buggy—shucks! perambulator, I meant—where he lies kicking his legs about, ready to defend himself with his flailing arms, having realized that, dammit, he's a citizen of this country too, that he has the rights to (a) deny any bubble entry into his fortress, and (b) say to this woman (whose painted claws are now an inch away from my eye), "Get lost, go to hell, leave my buddy and Ms. Oates alone, and get the fuck out of here before I call security, you heartless, ruthless shit!"

About the Author

Heather O'Shea Gordon

What she remembers of Ireland
is sheep, blanketing the hills
and peat fires and how it felt
to wear two sweaters on the sea.

She wore wool
mittens in Maynooth
remembers ladies selling scarves
and chickens from carts
on Grafton Street.

In England she ate scones
in Canterbury, envied schoolboys,
was disappointed by Oxford
and loved the Thames.

Before that it was mostly Pennsylvania.
She lived on Marvle Valley
with three sisters, two brothers,
her parents and a cat.
She remembers painting
with potatoes and chokecherries,
loving a hawthorn,
wanting windowsills.

She calls herself, alternately,
daughter, sister, lover, friend.
Living in New Mexico
she drives red mesas
and finds the altitude confusing.

When the moon is close
she cannot tell
which clouds rise up
and which press down.

WHEN I DREAM NANCY SPUNGEN*

Michael Sinclair

I

Last week I read to a room of tilted heads
half the age of mine. Your dark poetry, one guy said,
is not girl-getting. I said good point. Next guy
asks why a man thirty-eight writes his childhood.
I say good for you that's a damned good question.

II

She moaned Ma into the payphone. I need money.
Sell my stocks, what Gramma left. Okay. Talk to Sid: *Hullo.*
Sid loves you Ma we're clean now, back on fuckin methadone.

Sid played with the thumbtack run through her ear.
She strummed her painted nail on his fly. They're my bonds,
bitch, put Daddy on the phone. *Manny, come here.* Yeah Ma, why?

He's not asleep, I heard what he said. Sid loves me more
on weekends than you guys ever did. Send me the money,
wire it tonight. Or I'm back on junk *Both of us* and we're dead.

III

I knew this girl when I was fifteen. Her hair,
she dyed a bruisy blue. I remember her name now:
Carol. There was a knot of us, maybe ten. We
all did acid and downers together:

**Nancy was knifed by her lover, a Sex Pistol, Sid Vicious.
She bled and was buried in a prom dress.*

that and sex and something wedged
between each of us and our parents, who were surgeons,
mechanics, or hypnotists, strangers one to the other,

kept us within arm's reach, day and night,
for months. Carol battered

the paint-spattered upright piano
(its hammers had been tipped with thumbtacks).
She barked a song called *George*.
The lyric was *George*, nothing else.

Today I'd slap her sensible or call
911. Back then I thought
George was gorgeous, and meant

something. Today you'd say
Carol was borderline. Yesterday

she was the best of us, the knifeline,

our dangerous bloody future.

IV

I'd wake in a nest of bodies
smelling less of ferment
in the mouth of sleep
than of new sex: oatmeal and bleach.
I woke to call the day done,
pushed ahead back again to the dusk
of nembutal and black hashish.

V

There were sores at her hairline,
still pink from bleach. Sid walked
behind her because this was a day
Nancy was in charge.
I'm hungry (it was his day

to plead), he pled near the clinic door.
Food he didn't need. His need
was Nancy against him, covering
the length of him, every spot,
her skin on his. Sid
if you eat you'll just puke it up.

VI

Veteran's Village sold shoes: forty cents
a pair. You could wear shoes
new each day though used,
if this were the past and you had money you didn't have then.
You, in the tossed clothes of a man
who now is mud

or one bud on a juniper
stacked in the Shriner's Fund Tree Lot.
Clothes dropped for resale
after burial and trumpetsong.
Clothes new to you
and good enough for another man to work a lifetime to buy.

VII

This scene is Anya and me: prattling
in the alcove about how the others
have changed so in twenty years:

Wil has lost his hair. Teri shrunk
her nose. Janet dropped the Planet
from her name. Albert is Al

but no taller, still unbathed.
That smoky catch in Denise's throat
is now fully blown. Diana drinks

a pitiful lot. I bring up Carol.
No one remembers *George* ,

the song she wrote, one word,

for that tinny piano.

VIII

Straight and dry after such a long time,
it's hard to be touched
when straight and dry.
I asked Norma after a month
to rub my stomach, no lower.
I could
       say I cried, but that's
not true. I wanted to, that's
enough for now.
               Love with her her
odor
is the tight adherence to daily
ritual I once had in drink and pills. I see Nancy Spungen

IX

laid out in Larchmont. The morgue stylist
has dyed her hair back brown. Nancy in polyester,
the prom dress cut out at the navel. Sid
killed her so he's not invited
to this wake. Her flesh
already collapsing, it will
soon be what it's meant to be,
but that dress won't rot
underground. Made in a mill,
it never will make new earth.

Modern Love I

Robert Burlingame

1) Almost no word is
worth the writing down.
Living, candid breath is better.
You ask me why. I say: Ask the sunrise.
But then what would spoken words do at
this moment except prattle about weather?

2) A small gray fox
comes into your clearing.
You want to feed it,
to see how delicately she eats.
But, a true fox, she won't stay.

3) A lifetime, says Buddha,
is like a flash of lightning, or
a torrent rushing down a steep
canyon. On this rainy afternoon,
close to the mountain, we confront these analogies.

4) You don't need my words
because you're in love with another
man. Your life is your life,
after all. Gates close. Gates open.
I loved you. Now it's all in your diary.

5) The problem is childhood,
those shrieks of a forgotten
morning. Sad childhood that wasn't
a childhood. On some high stage
this should be chanted, even into the darkness.

MODERN LOVE II

Robert Burlingame

1) As if we could say it outright. Still,
don't you know we find out as we go along,
our school days an abysmal misleading?
Together we stand under leaves,
thousands of leaves, gray oak leaves.
they speak their own tongue.

2) We will never see the loss we are,
gaunt ravine ingested by an old culvert,
place where the dead coyote lies,
slaughtered, dishevelled, its guts ribboning the rocks.
The wind takes its rotting fur,
then takes a little more.

3) Slowly we turn away, realize,
sing our knowledge in a music no one
has time or mind to hear.
It's like the music of some shy grove,
breeze in a pale dawn's ponderosa—
song drowned out by our day's idlest communings.

PAVANE

Jeanne Shannon

Pink light
under the new
hydrangea,
its green buds
swelling.

Jacqueline Kennedy
is dead.

◆

It's Newport, 1947,
the night of the Debutante Ball.

Jackie is coming down the stairs,
arms raised,
exultant,
laughing.

She's Deb of the Year
in her 59-dollar, off-the-rack dress.
She's Destiny's darling.
She's the Queen of Summer,
the Queen of the Milky Way.

◆

Newport, September
1953.

"I want,
more than
anything in the world,
to be married to him."

◆

At the Embassy party,
a stunning woman,
another one of Jack's amours.

Jackie is nervous.
She's wearing her hair up.
Her hairpins keep falling out.

◆

1994,
the twenty-third
afternoon of May.

Across the Potomac,
cathedral bells
ring 64 times.

Birds are singing
from all the trees.

◆

A young woman says,

> I wasn't even born then,
> but I had to be here.
>
> She was a mystery.
> That whole era
> was a mystery.
>
> But this is the end
> of what happened to them.
>
> This is the closing
> of a door.

✦

The sweet May sunlight
above the graves.

How different the weather was,
that lonesome Monday
in November.

✦

Sun in Leo,
Moon in Aries.

Where has she gone,
the Queen of Summer,

with her Sun and Moon
in the signs of Fire?

DIMENSIONS *Bret Streeter*

BOOK REVIEWS

Helen Keller or Arakawa, by Madeline Gins. (Santa Fe, NM: Burning Books with New York: East-West Cultural Studies, 1994), 309 pages, $29.50. Distribution Information: D.A.P. (Distributed Art Publishers) 1-800-338-BOOK.

Megan Simpson

"Here begins the practicing by a blank plasticity of a guerilla epistemology." This sentence, occurring near the end of Madeline Gins' latest work of prose, in a discussion among a philosopher, a horticulturist, an architect and two artists about pruning a branch from an enormous pine tree, perfectly describes my experience of reading this text. *Helen Keller or Arakawa* (beautifully designed by Burning Books' Michael Sumner) defies conventions of genre so radically, and is so utterly unlike anything I have ever read, that I find myself as attentive to *how* I'm reading as to *what* I'm reading. My most familiar, tried-and-true methods of literary comprehension give way to the new. But this, after all, is part of the point.

Gins, long-time collaborator with painter Arakawa (their collaborations include large-scale architectural installations as well as written and printed works), considers eighty-six of the artist's abstract works in her book while simultaneously conducting a rigorous and playful inquiry into the nature of spacetime, perception, subjectivity, and language. Often narrated in the persona of Helen Keller, taken from her diaries, the book constantly shifts point of view, proceeding by way of monologue and dialogue among such characters as Helen, "a subjectively mediated, objective quality," physicist Niels Bohr, an imaginary physicist/philosopher named Ivor Plenum ("plenum" refers to the notion held by stoic philosophers that all of space is filled with matter), a beach, and Anne Sullivan (Helen's teacher). Although the richly layered text submits to no overt narrative structure, Gins makes extensive use of narrative in the form of brief metaphysical fables. She draws on a range of printed sources throughout the book's twenty-nine short chapters, appropriating and integrating text by art critics, Zen masters, poets, philosophers and physicists. The result, a multi-dimensional, multi-disciplinary collage, presents a convincing argument against the normative modes of perception, thought and being through which we limit our human potential.

Gins insists that perception—not surprisingly a key concern for a writer schooled in philosophy, physics and art—is not merely reflective, but is the means by which we create art ("What in line draws itself along and through as line if not the perceiving of it?"), the world, and ultimately ourselves. Helen explains, "I could not, it seems, form myself without first having formed the world." In addition, our encounter with the world is not fixed in the metaphysical vacuum of phenomenology; Gins insists that "the limits of perception are not absolute but are a function of an historically determined code that can be changed." And herein lies our hope for the future.

Throughout *Helen Keller or Arakawa*, Gins suggests that we can change the codes that limit perception, and thereby achieve "critical expansiveness," by transgressing supposed boundaries and deconstructing false oppositions that reign in Western discourse and thought. The first such boundary to go is that which separates art from lived experience. As Gins writes, "[w]henever Helen Keller writes of her experiences, she invariably ends up describing an Arakawa painting." In addition, sight is not the opposite of blindness, for sight itself can limit vision, acting as a "cutting-off maneuver." Without sight Helen is allowed "the option of a wide-open focus." Other oppositions Gins questions include mysticism/pragmatism, concreteness/ abstraction, blankness/volume, place/no place, thick/thin.

Perhaps the most persistent challenge Gins makes in this text is directed at the distinction between self and not-self. Gins' reconfiguration of the subject is more radical than mere postmodern fragmentation, and fragmentation itself is not presented in her text as symptomatic of alienation. On the contrary, Helen's experience of herself as a "living canvas," "a swarm of living points," "*almost individual*," continuous both with the world and other people, encourages us to seek our own capacities for plurality and collectivity. Oneself as well as one's ideas are (or should be) realized as communal: ". . . the point that you see or make is not yours, not yours alone with which to do as you please."

I don't mean to imply that *Helen Keller or Arakawa* is dogmatic or pedantic. It is a dynamic and playful book, subtly persuasive, and rich with unexpected pleasures. Some highlights include Niels Bohr and Helen on the deck of an ocean liner heading for Japan, discussing (with their hands) color and protoplasm; an entire chapter, called "Birds," devoted to the phoneme "th"; papers presented at the First Annual Conference of Architecture and the Deafblind (1996) reprinted in their entirety as chapter twenty-five; Helen's acquisition of the word "love"; and an extended meditation on the "Shinnyu" radical, "an element in the first of two characters making up the word for reason in Japanese. . . . Taken alone, the first character of this pair is the word for path or way; it is the Tao."

This is a book that, although difficult at first, teaches the reader how to read it. The strange becomes familiar, and certain initially-puzzling terms which recur throughout the book—"perceptual landing sites," "projective envelopes"—become clear and meaningful. "Transitivity," for example, is a grammatical concept that Gins extends beyond language and into the realm of human thought and action: "To be transitive is to have carry-over onto something else." *Helen Keller or Arakawa* possesses this valuable quality of transitivity: the modes of perceiving and thinking it initiates carry well beyond the reading of the book and into one's encounter with the world. After all, in the words of Karl Marx, as quoted by Gins, "We have sufficiently explained the world, the *point* is to transform it."

DOWNCAST EYES: THE DENIGRATION OF VISION IN TWENTIETH-CENTURY FRENCH THOUGHT (NON-FICTION), MARTIN JAY. (BERKELEY: UNIVERSITY OF CALIFORNIA PRESS, 1994), 643 PAGES, $16.00

Anne Foltz

Martin Jay's *Downcast Eyes: The Denigration of Vision in Twentieth-Century French Thought* is an extremely thorough and scholarly work, exploring the history of the visual from the Greeks to the present day, with a special emphasis on contemporary French theorists. What makes this book outstanding is not simply its vast scope, but the intricate detail which Jay brings to bear on the subject as a whole. Much more than a mere history of the visual arts, this work is a complete explication of the role of vision in formulating notions of epistemological and political discourse.

Jay moves from Plato through the Enlightenment to the Impressionists and Bergson to situate responses and reactions of 20th Century French theorists. He is able to discuss many of the figures considered to be central to postmodernism and/or poststructuralism with a depth and clarity which is rare in most theoretical writing. Some of the figures under consideration are Bataille, Sartre, Lacan, Althusser, Foucault, Barthes, Derrida, Irigaray, and Lyotard.

For example, as Bataille's current critical reception widens, Jay's consideration of Bataille is particularly noteworthy. Jay is able to consider Bataille's pornographic inclinations without ever diminishing the body of his contribution to 20th Century thought as a whole. Many theoretical texts allude to the problematic nature of Bataille's *oeuvre*, yet these discussions are seldom as frank and candid as presented here.

Downcast Eyes is both quite accessible and engaging, (here Jay does not suffer from the excessive and cryptic coding common to many recent theorists) though it is, however, not a book to be subjected to random "sampling" as Jay tends to invent and build upon a vocabulary as the work proceeds. The incredible number of cited authorities in the form of footnotes—ranging from one-quarter to one-half of each full page—tends to create a fairly interesting subtext, its own brand of denigration of the visual, and might, for some readers, be a bit overwhelming.

Many of Jay's conclusions regarding the field of the visual have parallels which can be applied to the broader pursuit of a definition of postmodernism and post-structuralism. As Jay regards Surrealism, he notes:

Still, what allows historians (and allowed its adherents) to call Surrealism a relatively coherent phenomenon suggests that at least some recurrent patterns can be discerned, which with due caution can be called typical.

Still further declaiming the importance of the study of the visual, Jay notes, "... a welter of overlapping attitudes, arguments, and assumptions shared by a large number of otherwise disparate thinkers has become apparent as never before." These two statements are precisely what constitutes primary current critical theoretical concerns—recurrent patterns of overlapping attitudes and arguments which are shared by such a complex, and not always congruent, body of theorists. The study of the individuals who constitute this "relatively coherent phenomenon" seems to be the only possible manner in which to investigate or inquire into postmodernism.

Jay has undertaken to examine these recurrent patterns which "... in all their rich and contradictory variety can still provide us mere mortals with insights and perspectives, speculations and observations, enlightenments and illuminations ...." This type of analysis would seem to be the vantage point from which to view and, hopefully, expand the complex and enigmatic nature of contemporary theoretical study.

GEORGES BATAILLE, BY MICHAEL RICHARDSON. (LONDON: ROUTLEDGE, 1994), 148 PAGES, $49.95, CLOTH; $16.95, PAPER.

Jennifer Timoner

Michael Richardson's critical study of Georges Bataille, which endeavors "to place Bataille's work in sociological perspective," serves as a fairly clear and not uninteresting introduction to some of the major concerns and texts of the often exalted and frequently marginalized French thinker. The 1980s saw a proliferation of English translations of Bataille's works, and Richardson's book is the first in English to scan the whole of these works in an attempt to extract the defining characteristics of Bataille's "philosophy", thus, it places itself at the necessary base of what should one day become a fertile space of critical inquiry.

In his introduction, Richardson examines the context in which Bataille is commonly explored: as a progenitor of postmodern philosophers, particularly Foucault, Derrida, and Baudrillard. Richardson argues that such exploration is misleading, and that to see Bataille through the postmoderns "is to emasculate what is original in his work." Although he notes with some pleasure the postmoderns' fascination with Bataille, Richardson claims that in their hands Bataille becomes "vulgarized" or misrepresented, and in any case, he asserts, it is always unwise to forget or dismiss the social and historical contexts of a text.

Richardson's next two brief chapters address Bataille's life and intellectual background, and also provide a kind of dictionary of recurring themes. Chapter Two, the five-page synopsis of Bataille's life includes what for me is the most illuminating biographical moment in the book. Richardson writes that in 1917, at the age of twenty, Bataille "had joined the seminary of Saint-Fleur with the intention of becoming a priest or a monk. Three years later, he tells us, he lost his faith and his vocation during a stay at a Benedictine monastery in the Isle of Wright because 'his Catholicism caused a woman he loved to shed tears'." Chapter Three begins with an extraordinarily useful discussion of those people who influenced Bataille—those from whom he culls certain ideas and against whom he endlessly pits himself. Richardson briefly but clearly explains the relation of Bataille's philosophy to those of Durkheim—who, according to Richardson, "provides the starting-point for Bataille's own sociology," Hegel, Marx, Sade, the Surrealists, and, importantly, Nietzsche:

For Bataille, Nietzsche was less a philosopher than a friend, or perhaps a sort of spiritual guide, someone to whom he could turn when things became difficult: all of his work is essentially a conversation with the German thinker. It is perhaps not accurate to speak of influence here, for it was really a question of love.

The chapter concludes with a helpful, though limited, glossary of "the key words" in Bataille's thought. Richardson provides for the fledgling reader the basic meanings and contexts of such notions as the sacred, communication, transgression, death, anguish, the impossible, and sovereignty—all of which take on meaning and significance quite particular to Bataille.

Setting Bataille's work in relation to both traditional scholarship and surrealism, "Towards a sociology of abundance" examines the methodology and fundamental urges and beliefs that underlie Bataille's production. Reacting against orthodox scientific method, which "involves the separation of knowing subject from unknowing object and abstracts the object of study from the totality of social relations," and working from the basic tenets of surrealism, Bataille develops the idea of "inner experience," which for him is the core of knowledge. As Richardson states, Bataille believes that "what one need[s] to examine more than anything . . . [is] one's own inner sense in relation to social reality." Readers who have yet to dig into Bataille's own writings will have to take Richardson at his word here, because although the concept of the inner experience does indeed define much of Bataille's textual production, Richardson fails, in my estimation, to provide enough direct source material to bring this notion to life.

In his next chapter Richardson delves into Bataille's economic theories, which challenge traditional economic theories that are based on the assumptions that there exists a scarcity of resources and that human nature seeks to accumulate wealth. He notes that for Bataille human nature is actually given to expenditure and that in fact, as Bataille writes, "The world . . . is sick with wealth." Richardson clearly summarizes, "In so far as there is poverty in the world, it is not caused by a scarcity of economic means but by the fact that one person's surplus has been appropriated by another." A thorough critique of the anthropological data on which Bataille bases his economic theories serves to highlight the weaknesses and many strengths of the writer's conception of the general economy, and Richardson is careful to be fair in his assessment of some of Bataille's more objective—and thus potentially questionable—analyses.

As Richardson notes, "Bataille was determined to explore the very heart of things." The final chapter, "Death, communication, and the experience of limits," deals with Bataille's work on sexuality and religion. Richardson concisely summarizes many of Bataille's major concerns in these areas, beginning with his beliefs about death (the recognition of which "results in the sentiment of eroticism") and continuing with taboo and transgression. Richardson explains that for Bataille,

> Transgression was ... an essential component of ... taboo. It did not stand outside it, nor was the impulse behind transgression to subvert the taboo but on the contrary to ensure its effectiveness. Transgression, therefore, 'does not deny the taboo, but transcends and completes it'.

Richardson goes on to explicate Bataille's attitude toward and work on Christianity, and concludes that:

> one does not get the impression that he had renounced Christianity because he felt it to be oppressive. It was rather a sense of disappointment: Christianity was unable to satisfy his need for the absolute ... it was unable to give him a framework to come to terms with the intensity of his religious feelings. Christianity was too complacent. It was, in fact, not religious enough. It represented a poverty of existence not, as a religion should, its abundance.

Richardson concludes his book with the suggestion that, although Bataille engages ruthlessly with anguish and uncertainty, we should remember that he also insisted that laughter was always the appropriate response to the pains of existence.

As an introduction to the life and work of Georges Bataille, Richardson's book is clear and accessible. However, I found myself craving even a bit of the utter intensity of feeling and imagination that characterize Bataille's writing; Richardson seems to lack the enthusiasm so evident in Bataille. Although this study offers readers new to Bataille helpful background information, I cannot help but wonder if it might discourage some people by failing to convey a real sense of the power and vehemence of Bataille's thought. Richardson truly shortchanges both his readers and Bataille when he dismisses works like "The Solar Anus" as bearing "witness to [Bataille's] disturbed state" or notes only that Bataille's beautiful work *The Impossible* "is a very strange book indeed." Richardson succumbs to the temptation to gloss over Bataille's less "rational" texts and disappointingly contends that, for example, his novels "need to be considered as the negative underside" of his more traditional sociological or philosophical work. Although Richardson posits, as the final word in his book, that students of Bataille must engage with the whole of his production because "his fragments and rambling ruminations are often as important as his more coherently developed work," he does not follow his own suggestion, and the study suffers for it. Bataille begins his preface to *On Nietzsche* thus: "Motivating this writing—as I see it—is fear of going crazy." Richardson never allows us to glimpse the depth of that fear.

WEATHERING   *Bret Streeter*

CONTRIBUTOR'S NOTES

Jefferson Adams holds degrees in philosophy and creative writing from Arizona State University (ASU). He has taught English at South Mountain College and Mesa College. He received residency fellowships from the Helene Wurlitzer Foundation and the Villa Montalvo Center for the Arts. Poems from his full-length collection, *Pisces in Flight*, have appeared recently in *Antioch Review, CALIBAN, Mississippi Review, Hayden's Ferry Review*, and the *South Ash Press*, among others. He lives in Northern California where he is currently seeking both a publisher and a job.

Craig M. Baehr is a graduate student in the writing program at the University of New Mexico(UNM). He also works full time as an Engineering Tech/Editor for the U.S. Government, and has been named poetry editor for UNM's upcoming issue of *Conceptions Southwest*. Craig's works have appeared in *New Mexico English Journal, Conceptions Southwest* and *Man, Alive*!

Joanna Brooks is a graduate student in English at UCLA where she holds the Battrick Fellowship for poetry. Her fiction and poetry has, or will soon appear in *ZYZZYVA, South Dakota Review, Dialogue*, and elsewhere. She is a proud fourth-generation Los Angeleno. Her late grandfather, who grew up downtown, once told her that when the L.A. River flooded in the 1920s, the city health department paid kids for each rat they killed. In her spare time, Joanna enjoys boxing.

Robert Burlingame, Emeritus Professor of English at the University of Texas at El Paso, lives on a ranch in the Guadalupe Mountains, where he also volunteers at the National Park. His work has appeared in numerous publications throughout the United States, Canada and South America, and he is working on a group of new poems.

Bobby Byrd is a poet. For the last several years he has felt surrounded by fiction writers, so he began writing short stories as an aberrant excursion, his anger serving as motivator. Last summer he spent two months in Mexico as a participant in the National Education Association's International Program. He and his wife (a fiction writer) are co-publishers of Cinco Puntos Press in El Paso.

Tina Carlson is an avid mountain climber, a home health-care nurse, and a graduate student in creative writing at UNM.

Albino Carrillo grew up in Albuquerque, attended UNM, and took an MFA in creative writing from ASU. His poems have recently appeared in the *Antioch Review*, the *Midwest Quarterly, Sou'Wester*, and other small magazines. He currently teaches creative writing at Union College in Schenectady, New York.

Jeffrey Lamar Coleman is working toward his PhD in American Studies at UNM. His dissertation topic is the poetry of the Civil Rights Movement. Jeffrey earned his MFA in creative writing at ASU, where he had the great fortune of serving as co-editor for two issues of *Hayden's Ferry Review*, the literary magazine of ASU.

John Couturier grew up in Evergreen, Colorado, and Washington, D.C., and now lives in Brooklyn, New York. He has worked in retail, banking, and publishing. Currently, he is a volunteer tutor in the adult literacy program at the Brooklyn Public Library. His poems have appeared in a variety of small magazines, most recently, *Black Fly Review, Brooklyn Review, New York Quarterly,* and *Pearl*.

Robert Edwards' work has appeared in several literary magazines, and his list of published books includes *Radio Venceremos* (1990) *Nixies* (1993) and *A Trick of the Light* (1993).

José Esquinas was born in Puerto Rico, raised in Mexico, Distrito Federal, and currently resides in Santa Fe, New Mexico. His fiction has appeared in *Bilingual Review/Revista Bilingue, Saguaro, Chiricu,* and *Descant*. He earns his living as a translator and interpreter of Spanish.

Carrie Etter has work forthcoming in the *Beloit Poetry Journal*, the *Laurel Review*, and the *Literary Review*. Carrie teaches in the commmunity services programs at Santa Monica College and she often can be seen skating on the path between Malibu and Venice Beach, California.

Miguel Gandert is a native of Española, New Mexico, and a research associate at the Southwest Hispanic Research Institute/Center for Regional Studies at UNM. Miguel's photos have been shown in numerous galleries throughout the United States and the world. His work was selected (including some of the photos in this issue) for a 1993 exhibition at the Whitney Museum in New York City.

Jana Giles spent her childhood on the east side of the Sandia Mountains (central New Mexico) and has lived in Puerto Rico, Maryland, and Chile. Jana earned her Master of Arts degree in creative writing from the University of New Mexico in 1994, and currently she is working on her PhD in 20th-Century literature, reading Samuel Beckett, teaching freshman composition, and wishing she had more time to work on her novel.

Heather O'Shea Gordon is originally from Bethel Park, Pennsylvania, a suburb of Pittsburgh. She graduated from the University of Notre Dame with a bachelor of arts degree in English, economics and theology. Heather's next academic endeavor brought her to UNM, where she first earned an MBA, and currently is pursuing a master's degree in English, hoping to graduate in 1995.

Jenny Goldberg lives in Taos, New Mexico, where she writes poetry, essays, and short fiction. A writer, editor and camera operator for several public broadcasting stations, she directed and filmed a prizewinning documentary called *The Homefront*, distributed by Third World Newsreel.

C. John Graham lives in Santa Fe and is an environment, safety and health team leader for the accelerator division at Los Alamos National Laboratory. He edits poetry for *The Santa Fe Sun*, and is a member of the clergy of Eckankar.

Gabriel Herrera will graduate from high school in El Paso, Texas, this spring and is deciding on a university where he will continue his education in creative writing. He wrote "No Me Gusta el Chile" while attending the Summer Writer's Workshop in Santa Fe. Gabriel organized a first-ever poetry reading at his high school last year, expecting 20-30 attendants. More than 300 people turned out for the event.

Criss Jay received his BA in English from UCLA and went on to teach writing at Ohlone College and San Francisco State University, where he did his graduate work in American Literary Studies. A collection of his poems, *A World Insomnia of Poems*, was issued as a chapbook by his own Blue Meadow Press. His work has appeared in *Blue Mesa Review, Tamaqua,* and *Poet* magazine.

Sören Johnson is a poet from New Mexico, where he studied at St. John's College and at the University of New Mexico. Sören now lives in Amsterdam, where he teaches English to Dutch businessmen, as well as writing classes at the Free University. He has traveled widely and continues to live in wonder with the world. His poetry has been published in *Carolina Quarterly, Puerto del Sol, Another Chicago Magazine,* and recently in the U.K. in *Orbis International* and *Iota*.

Trebbe Johnson's essays, articles and poetry focus on the relationship between land and spirituality. Her work has appeared recently in *Harper's, New Age, Parabola, Boulevard,* and on National Public Radio. Her documentary video, "Only One Earth," produced for the United Nation's twentieth anniversary celebration of Earth Day, won a Telly award.

Mary Helen Fierro Klare is a professional musician and a bilingual writer of poetry, fiction and nonfiction. Born and raised in El Paso, Texas, she received a master's degree in music education from the University of Colorado. She recently completed a manuscript of Spanish poetry entitled *Poemas de un Libro Azul*. Mary teaches orchestra in Los Alamos public schools where she has lived since 1969, yet remains "absorbed in the daily rediscovery of Northern New Mexico's spectacular beauty."

Laurie Kutchins' book of poetry *Between Towns* was published in 1993 by Texas Tech University Press. Laurie, who spent most of her life in Casper, Wyoming, teaches creative writing at James Madison University.

Karla Kuyaca is a native of San Francisco, where she sometimes read her poetry in the North Beach area in the 1960s. Since then she has pursued other artistic mediums, but derives the most satisfaction from writing. Karla recently graduated from the creative writing program at the Institute of American Indian Arts in Santa Fe.

Enrique R. Lamadrid is a long time Alburqueño who teaches ethnopoetics, Chicano literature, Coyote studies, and the mythology of Querencia in the Department of Spanish & Portuguese at UNM. In 1994 he published *Tesoros del Espíritu: A Portrait in Sound of Hispanic New Mexico* (Albuquerque: Academia/El Norte), the first aural history of Nuevomexicano culture.

Erika Lenz is an MFA candidate at ASU, where she spent the last year as poetry editor of *Hayden's Ferry Review*. She also works part time as a freelance writer, and has articles forthcoming in *The Bloomsbury Review, Controlled Burn* and *Mid-American Review*.

Lyn Lifshin has published several books including *Black Apples, Upstate Madonna, Kiss the Skin Off* and *Not Made of Glass*, and has edited four anthologies of women's writing including *Ariadne's Thread* from Harper and Row and *Tangled Vines* from Beacon Press. She is the subject of a documentary film, "Lyn Lifshin: Not Made of Glass;" she lectures and gives readings widely and has been published in many magazines including *Ms., American Poetry Review,* and *Rolling Stone*. Her newest book is *The Marilyn Monroe Poems* from Quiet Lion Press.

Glenna Luschei is an avocado rancher and a poet in California. She also works part time as a medical interpreter for farm workers. A publisher for thirty years, she is helping to fund a women's cooperative called "Angels" in Albuquerque, New Mexico.

E.A. Mares, poet, playwrite, historian and gearshift-knob connessiuer, Mares was born and raised in Albuquerque's Old Town. He presently teaches English at the Univeristy of North Texas in Denton. In the autumn of 1995 he will join the English Department at UNM, where (when he was a student) he was a Students for a Democratic Society organizer.

Robert Masterson lives in Albuquerque, New Mexico. As a teacher, he has worked for UNM, the Albuquerque Public Schools system, the Ministry of Education of the People's Republic of China, and both the Colorado and New Mexico prison systems. He owns and operates Lords of Language, which sponsors a wide variety of literary events and publishes both the literary/arts magazine *Manila* and the *American Poetry Contemporary Writing Series* of books.

Mario Materassi is a professor of American Literature at the University of Florence, Italy. For work as well as for sheer pleasure, he and his family are "enchanted with New Mexico." He published an interview with Bharati Mukherjee (*The Tiger's Daughter*), in issue number five of *Blue Mesa.*

Carl Mayfield wanders around near his home on the fringes of Albuquerque; always bald, often sober, prone to spontaneous meditations on anything that comes along. His poems have been published in a variety of magazines over several lifetimes, including *Blue Mesa Review.* He has two books in print: *Sandia Mountain Sequence* and *Circling the Garden/A Moon Walk* (the latter with Baker Morrow). Mayfield writes poetry because ". . . it's the only examination my eggshell ego will allow without bouts of extreme grumpiness."

Cathryn McCracken lives in Albuquerque. Her poetry has appeared in *Blue Mesa Review, Chelsea, Xanadu, Exit 13* and *Up Against the Wall, Mother,* among others. She was most recently published in the bilingual anthology, *Saludos-Poemas de Nuevo Mexico.* She is also a graduate student in the creative writing program at UNM and is at work completing her first novel.

Jennifer Miller recently received a master's degree in English fromUNM, after completing semesters abroad in Scotland and Mexico. Her work has appeared in *Bughouse, Manila* and *Conceptions Southwest.*

Pauline Mounsey is a native of Nebraska who has lived in Phoenix, Arizona since 1965. She has directed the Divergent Arts Poetry Series (monthly featured readings) for the past five years and hosts and directs a television poetry program, "Visual Voices," which airs weekly. She is also the managing editor of a new national poetry quarterly, *The Lucid Stone.* While writing and getting published, she has also taught in one-room school houses, hiked the Grand Canyon and flown in open-cockpit planes.

Enid Osborn is a native of New Mexico who now resides in Santa Barbara, California. A graduate of UNM, Enid writes songs, poetry, short stories and essays. She is interested in the preservation of human rights as well as open spaces, which are rapidly disappearing on the West Coast. This is her third time to be published in *Blue Mesa Review.*

Joe Pitkin lives in Las Cruces, New Mexico, with his wife and daughter. Las Cruces is also home to New Mexico State University where Joe works on his MA in English, and edits the Spanish-language contributions to the department's literary magazine, *Puerto del Sol.*

Iqbal Pittalwala came to the United States from Bombay, India. He has published short stories in the *Seattle Review, Wascana Review, North Atlantic Review* and others. He teaches rhetoric at the University of Iowa, where he expects to graduate with an MFA in fiction from the Iowa Writers' Workshop in May, 1995.

V.B. Price is a poet and journalist interested in the connection between culture, ecology, and the imagination. His latest books are a collection of poems entitled *Chaco Body* (Artspace Press, 1991), and *A City At The End Of The World* (UNM Press, 1991). He is the co-editor with Baker Morrow of the soon to be published *Anasazi Architecture and American Design* (UNM Press, 1996). Price teaches in the UNM General Honors Program and in the School of Architecture and Planning.

Henry Rael, Jr. has an MA in English from UNM. He is currently pursuing a career in screenwriting, living and working in Los Angeles, California.

Harvena Richter works in fiction and nonfiction, but poetry is her main source of pleasure. A collection titled *"The Yaddo Elegies and other Poems,"* will be published this year.

Alexis Rotella is the author of 34 books of poetry, most of them haiku and other forms of Japanese poetry. In 1987 she became the first American woman to publish a collection of tanka. During the summer of 1994 one of her senryu poems, which appeared in the *New York Times* and the *New Yorker,* also was displayed on a Forty-Second Street marquee in New York City. That year her poems were aired over several public radio stations across the country. When she is not writing, Alexis practices as an interfaith minister and counselor.

Megan Simpson's poems and prose have appeared in *Black Warrior Review, Five Fingers Review, Mirage,* and *Kayak.* Currently she is a graduate student in English at UNM, writing her doctoral dissertation on contemporary women writers.

Michael Sinclair was born near Newman, Illinois ("a blasted early youth"), married and worked various "messy" jobs (janitor, haircutter, "behavioral trainer") before earning his MFA in poetry and fiction from the University of Iowa in 1994. Currently, Sinclair assists at an Iowa City electoconvulsive therapy treatment facility, and teaches composition at the local community college to keep the wolves at bay while working on his book of poetry and "extra-quick fiction."

Jeanne Shannon lives in Albuquerque. Her work has appeared recently in *Now and Then, Cross Roads, Color Wheel,* and *Cafe Solo.* Her most recent chapbook of poetry is called *Dissolving Forms.*

William B. Smith graduated from UNM with his bachelor's degree in English in May 1995. His plans include traveling to and around Alaska "until my money runs out," at which time he would like to teach English at the high school or middle school level.

Glen Sorestad is a well known Canadian poet whose poems have appeared in literary magazines and journals across North America and in Europe. Among his eight books of poetry are *Air Canada Owls* (1990) and *West Into Night* (1991). He lives in Saskatoon, Saskatchewan.

Kathleen Spivack just finished a novel about the lives of refugee European intellectuals in New York City during WWII called *Unspeakable Things*. Her essay "Between Two Cultures" will be published this summer in the *Kenyon Review*. Originally from Boston, Kathleen spent the past four years in France teaching and writing at the Sorbonne on a Fulbright scholarship. A visiting professor at UNM, she was drawn to the land of enchantment because of "an interest in contemporary American literature produced in a multicultural environment."

Roberta Swann's poetry and fiction have recently appeared in *Ploughshares, North American Review, 13th Moon* and *New Letters*. Roberta is co-founder (with Gary Giddins and John Lewis) of the American Jazz Orchestra, which is celebrating its 40th anniversary this year.

Thomas Swiss teaches at Drake University. Poems from a recently completed manuscript will appear in *Boston Review, Agni Review, Iowa Review* and other journals. His first book, *Measure*, was recently published by the University of Alabama Press.

Jennifer Timoner is a graduate student in English at UNM.

Truong Tran has most recently had poems published in *Crazyhorse, North Dakota Quarterly, Berkeley Poetry Review* and *ZYZZYVA*. "My Father's Legacy" and "My Father's Story" are part of a collection entitled *Placing the Accents*, for which he is currently seeking a publisher. Troung spent the spring recovering from the California floods.

Sergio Troncoso was born in El Paso, Texas, and now lives in New York City. After graduating from Harvard University, he was a Fulbright Scholar in Mexico and received two graduate degrees from Yale University, where he now teaches. Sergio is writing a novel about moral murder and his work has recently appeared in the *Rio Grande Review, American Way,* and *Blue Mesa*.

Amy Uyematsu is a sansei (third-generation Japanese American) from Los Angeles. Her first book, *Thirty Miles from J-Town* (Story Line Press, 1992), won the 1992 Nicholas Roerich Prize. Recent work also appears in *Bakunin,* the *Asian Pacific American Journal,* and *I Am Becoming the Woman I've Wanted.*

Cody Wasner is a new writer, and *Drawing Blood* is his second published story. His first story (also about the medical profession) was published last year in *Mediphors*. Dr. Wasner practices rheumatology in Eugene, Oregon, where he lives with his wife, four children, two dogs, seven cats, five birds, and an iguana.

Peter Wild presently is studying the former boom town of Doggett, California, located in the Mojave Desert.

Leilani Wright lives in the Sonoran Desert in Mesa, Arizona with her daughter Hannah. Recent work has appeared in *Hayden's Ferry Review, Exquisite Corpse, The Dickinson Review,* and the *Christian Science Monitor*. A chapbook of her poetry titled *A Natural Good Shot* was published in 1994.